WORDS
IN MIND

WORDS IN MIND

An Affable Guide to

Building Vocabulary

Vicki Wilt
Alan Michael Wilt

Prior editions of this book were published as *Scholastic's A+ Guide to a Better Vocabulary* by Vicki Tyler.

ISBN: 978-0-9883727-2-6

Vicki Wilt was an educational writer and editor and the author of numerous fiction and nonfiction books for young people. She died in 2013.

Alan Michael Wilt is a writer and editor and is the author of *The Holy Family: A Novel*. He lives in western Massachusetts.

Contents

Special Features Guide

"Words words, words."

William
Shakespeare,
Hamlet

Chapter 1

Putting It into Words

Have you ever felt very confused about something, until you actually sat down and put your feeling into words—and then it turned out you weren't so confused after all? That's something that happens to a lot of people. Somehow, when we put our feelings into words—by talking to a friend, writing a blog, posting to a social network, writing in a diary, or whatever—we can sometimes find out things we didn't even know that we knew!

Or maybe this has happened to you: You're listening to a friend talk about something that happened to him or her, or you're reading a story, and suddenly you think, "I know *exactly* what she means" or "I've felt *exactly* the same way." Being able to put our feelings into words allows us to think about them in new ways and to share our discoveries with other people. It can also give us some feeling of control over our world.

Human beings love to communicate—to understand things and to be understood. Have you ever heard two people talking in a foreign language right in front of you, and felt very frustrated, like an outsider who didn't know what was going on? Or tried to read something in English that you couldn't quite understand because the words were too "hard"? One of the most frustrating feelings we experience is not being able to understand another person or make ourselves understood.

Words can help us understand the world, participate in the world, and influence the world. Words make progress possible. For example, scientists working today can build on the discoveries of scientists who came before them, because those past discoveries were written down in words. Anyone who can write can leave behind messages to future generations. Words are like a time machine that can carry us back to the past or carry our ideas into the future. The more you know about words, the better you can communicate with people and share their experiences—whether it's the person sitting next to you in study hall, someone on the other side of the world, someone who lived centuries before you were born, or some unknown person in the future who might come across the secret thoughts in your diary some day!

In a world of email, blogs, and text messages, words are more important than ever. Today, the click of a button can send your words speeding to readers around the world. That's why it's more important than ever to find the right words to say exactly what you mean.

Learning about language doesn't mean memorizing a bunch of "hard" words, though. It doesn't mean using a big word where a little word will do, either. It means *caring* about what you have to say, and caring about the people who are listening to you or reading your words. It means caring enough to try to use the best word in every situation—the word that's clear and interesting, rather than vague and boring; the word that will make your audience understand how you feel, laugh at your jokes, think about a problem you think is important, or simply pay attention to you.

After all, the right words can inspire love or hate, can make someone feel overjoyed or miserable or furious, can win an argument, or can even change the course of history. Remember, for example, that freedom in America is protected by words—the words of the United States Constitution and the Bill of Rights.

English, especially American English, is a fascinating language. Depending on your age, your interests, your education, what part of the country you live in, and who you're talking to, there are all kinds of ways to express the same idea. That's because American English has been created by people from a wide variety of backgrounds, and because the language is so alive—always growing and changing.

Where do words come from? Why are there so many of them—and some that mean almost the same thing? What do all those words have to do with you? In other words, why should you care about studying vocabulary?

Words Come from People's Experiences

People invent words because they need to name the things that they experience. The words people use tell us a lot about those people. Words tell us what people do, what they think about, what makes them laugh, what makes them angry, and what is most important in their world.

For example, after the Industrial Revolution, dozens of new words were coined to describe new conditions in people's lives, or old words acquired new meanings. People now worked in factories where they became known collectively as *labor* or *blue-collar* workers. They worked on *assembly lines* and formed *unions* to engage in *collective bargaining* with *management*. They demanded a *minimum wage* and *fringe benefits*. If collective bargaining failed, they organized *strikes*, *walk outs*, or *pickets*. Union members hated *scabs*, workers who dared to cross their picket lines. Factory workers feared *automation*, which increasingly replaced human labor with machines.

Today, as manufacturing increasingly gives way to the Information Age and a service economy, the words of the Industrial Age are fading, and dozens of new words are replacing them. For instance, today more workers sit at *keyboards* in *cubicles*, engaging in *word processing* or *data entry*, sending *emails*, designing *web sites*, or writing copy for *content mills* that demand *search engine optimization*. In this world, the most hated participants are *lurkers*, *spammers*, *flamers*, and *hackers*. We live in a new world that demands and inspires new words almost every day.

Where American English Comes From

The American vocabulary is especially rich and varied because our language, as well as our population, has come from many different sources. Besides the thousands of words from Anglo-Saxon, Latin, and Greek—the three main sources of English—we've also borrowed words from the following language sources:

> **French**: matinee, café, restaurant, chef, mayonnaise, cuisine, garage, rouge, sabotage
>
> **German**: delicatessen, frankfurter, kindergarten, pretzel, spiel
>
> **Italian**: opera, piano, staccato, virtuoso, alto, soprano, solo, mezzanine, arcade
>
> **Dutch**: boss, snoop, spook, stoop, waffle
>
> **Spanish**: bronco, lasso, ranch, canyon, mosquito, patio, plaza, tornado, macho
>
> **Hebrew**: amen, cinnamon, messiah, jubilee, hallelujah
>
> **African Languages**: banjo, gumbo, okra, tote, yam
>
> **Arabic**: alcohol, algebra, magazine, sofa, zero
>
> **Native American Languages:** moccasin, caribou, chipmunk, moose, opossum, pecan, raccoon, skunk, squash

Notice that the words we have taken from these foreign languages are often clues to the ways those countries or cultures have influenced us the most. For example, many of the borrowed French words have to do with food and cooking. Many of the Italian words have to do with music. Many of the Native American words are names for things that American colonists had never seen before they came to the New World. Two of the Arabic words have to do with mathematics, and several of the Hebrew words have to do with religion. And so on.

Words Stand for Ideas

The history of language is the history of what people have thought about. An idea cannot have any influence in the word until people give it a name. Once an idea has a name, people can talk about it. And after people talk about an idea for a while, it begins to seem natural, as if it always existed. The ancient Greeks had a new idea once upon a time. They thought that people should be free to choose their own leaders. They invented a word for this idea, *dēmokratia*, which in Greek means "rule by the people." The idea lives on today in our word *democracy*.

Other words that represent important ideas in history include *justice, equality, revolution, evolution, escape velocity, fission, gene, DNA, artificial intelligence*. You have studied or will study these words in your history or science classes. When you do, you'll discover that the word we attach to an idea often becomes as important as the idea itself.

Words Tell a Story

We don't know how every object and idea got its name in every language. But we do know how many English words

> ❦
>
> Words form the thread on which we string our experiences.
> —Aldous Huxley
>
> ❦

came to be. There are often interesting stories behind words. For example, adults often use the word *precocious* (pri-kō′-shəs) to refer to children who are very mature for their age. This English word actually comes from two Latin words: *prae*, meaning "before"; and *coquere*, meaning "cooked" or "ripened." So precocious children are ones who have been "cooked" or "ripened" before their time!

The word *candidate* also has an interesting history. It literally means "clothed in white." In ancient Rome, a man announced that he wanted to run for office by appearing in public in a pure white toga. The white toga was supposed to represent a man's pure, blameless life. It was supposed to be a sign that he could be trusted. Candidates for office today don't wear togas, but they, too, want us to believe that they can be trusted, so the name fits.

Let's look at another example: The word *bombast*, which means talk or writing that tries to sound important but really isn't, comes from the name for a kind of cotton padding that men used to stuff under their shirts to make their shoulders look broader. People saw a connection between that kind of padding and the kind of padding people added to their language, so they used the same word for both.

Many English words derive from the names of people. For example, the *guillotine*, used to behead people during the French Revolution, was named after Dr. Joseph Guillotin, who first suggested that France use this method of execution. The word *maverick*, which means someone who doesn't go along with the crowd, comes from the name of Samuel A. Maverick, a Texas rancher who didn't bother to put a brand on his cows the way everyone else did. Other words that derive from the names of people include:

boycott	saxophone
chauvinism	shrapnel
lynch	silhouette
mesmerize	volt
nicotine	watt
pasteurize	

If you want to play word detective, you can find the stories of the above words in a good dictionary, either in print or online.

Many words also come from the names of characters in literature. A *scrooge,* as you probably know, is someone who takes after Ebenezer Scrooge, the miserly character in the Dickens story *A Christmas Carol.* A *Romeo* is a man who enjoys great success with women. And a *Frankenstein* is anyone who is destroyed by his or her own creation.

Mythology is an especially rich source of words. How many of the following words and stories do you recognize?

atlas: Atlas was the leader of the Titans, who rebelled against the Greek god Zeus. After the rebellion failed, Zeus punished Atlas by making him carry the heavens on his shoulders for all eternity. Early artists showed Atlas carrying a huge globe on his shoulders. Map-makers began using these pictures of Atlas in the front of their books of maps. And soon books of maps began to be called atlases. Believe it or not!

berserk: Berserk was the name of a man in Norse mythology who was said to fight with the fury of a wild beast. We now say that anyone so carried away with anger that he is dangerous to friends and enemies alike has "gone berserk."

narcissist: (nar′ sə sist): Narcissus was a handsome young man who fell in love with his own reflection in a pool of water and drowned. A narcissist, therefore, is someone who is conceited and thinks only of himself or herself. (By the way, Echo was in love with Narcissus, but Narcissus was too busy looking at his own reflection to notice. Some simple research will reveal to you how her name became the word *echo*.)

tantalize: Tantalus was a king who offended Zeus and received a terrible punishment for his crime. He was placed up to his neck in water. Clusters of fruit hung over his head, but whenever he reached up to eat the fruit, the branches pulled back out of his reach. And whenever he stooped to drink from the lake, the water disappeared. So to *tantalize* people is to show them something tempting that they can't have.

Other words from mythology include *lethargy, nemesis, panic, fury, siren, mentor,* and *odyssey.* You can find their stories in any good collection of myths.

Words Change Meaning and Form

The meaning of a word may change over time. Some words gradually take on a more general meaning, while some take on a more specific meaning. Some words take on a stronger meaning than they had originally, and some take on a weaker meaning. And some words change so drastically that it's difficult to explain how the change in meaning occurred.

The word *mortify* used to have a stronger meaning than it does today. To mortify someone used to mean to kill them! Today, however, a person can be mortified (humiliated) and still survive.

The English word *snack* comes from a Dutch word meaning "bite." But early Americans didn't use the word to mean a bite to eat. To them, it meant the bite of a dog! And the word *gossip* used to mean a godparent or friend of the family. Then, gradually, it came to mean a person who knows someone's personal secrets—and spreads them around. So today we have the verb "to gossip," thanks to the bad reputation of those ancient godparents!

Today we use the word *journey* to refer to any long trip, but the word used to have a more specific meaning. It comes from the French word for *day*, and used to mean the distance a person could walk in a day—about twenty miles.

It's easy to understand how the meanings of *mortify, snack, gossip,* and *journey* could have gradually changed. But how can we explain the fact that *villain* used to mean farm worker? That *nice* used to mean ignorant? And that the word *girl* used to refer to either male or female children? How could the meanings of these words have changed so drastically? To find out, word detectives called etymologists study what people have written down throughout history. They try to trace how the meanings of words have gradually or suddenly changed.

Words Come and Go

Not only do the meanings of words change, but the words themselves change. Often familiar words become shortened. For example, most of us say *phone* instead of telephone, *ad* rather than advertisement, and *gym* instead of gymnasium.

Some words actually die out because there is no longer a need for them, or simply because people stop using them. Some English words that have become obsolete are *bellytimber*, which used to mean food; *merry-go-sorry*, which used to mean something that makes you feel happy and sad at the same time; and *mubble-fubbles*, which used to mean a feeling of sadness that comes over a person for no apparent reason. You'll find these and other "dead" words brought back to life in the book *Poplollies and Bellibones: A Celebration of Lost words* by Susan Kelz Sperling, and at the web site The Phrontistery: A Compendium of Lost Words:

http://phrontistery.info/clw.html

Some words gradually disappear, but new words are constantly being invented. Dictionary makers say that about 500 new general vocabulary words are added to the language every year. How are new words invented? Some new words are combinations of old words. Either two whole words can be combined (*dishwasher, homecoming, newspaper*), or parts of the two words can be combined to form a new word. Can you guess what two words were combined to form each of the following? (See the answers below.)

> smog
> brunch
> twirl
> flare
> chortle
> ginormous
> blog
> crowdfunding

Some new words are invented to name new inventions or ideas (*software, hologram, internet, DVD, social networking*). The mathematical term *googol* was actually invented by a nine-year-old boy, whose uncle, a mathematician, asked him what he would call the number 1 followed by one hundred zeroes! The developers of the search engine Google liked the sound of this word so much that they changed the spelling a little and used it for the name of their company to signify the great number of results their search program would find.

Other new words are imaginative new ways of saying the same old things people have always said. Slang words fall into this category. People are always dreaming up new ways to say they're angry (*mad, riled up, sore, steamed up, hot under the collar*) or that someone else is crazy (*bonkers, loco, wacko*). They get tired of calling familiar things such as money (*scratch, dough, bread, moolah, bills*) or food (*chow, grub*) by the same old names, so they make up new names. Some slang words have become a permanent part of the language, but many are forgotten in a few years as people get bored with them and replace them with even newer words. You'll learn more about slang in Chapter 6.

Answers
smog = smoke + fog
brunch = breakfast + lunch
twirl = twist + whirl
flare = flame + glare
chortle = chuckle + snort
blog = web + log
crowdfunding = crowd + funding

Here's Where You Come In

English is growing and changing every day because of *you*. The people who use a language are the ones who keep it alive—the ones who invent new words or new meanings for old words, and who sometimes allow important words to be lost by not using them at all or by not using them with care. To keep important ideas alive, the words that refer to those ideas must be kept alive and used carefully.

Keeping in touch with your language means keeping in touch with your world. To know what's going on, to really be a part of any group, you have to "speak their language." Whatever future you choose, the ability to use language carefully and imaginatively will be a big help to you. So start now. Be curious about words. Use them with care. And don't be afraid to play with them! That's how to keep the language—and the gray matter between your ears— alive!

Are You in Touch?

How many of the following recently invented words do you recognize?

crowdsourcing	buzzword	newbie
airball	dramedy	landline
binge-watch	fashionista	webinar
microbiome	widget	emoticon
photobomb	tweet	emoji
ping	staycation	hoodie
hotspot	netiquette	truthiness
microaggression	hacktivist	yowza

Invent Your Own Words

What do you call a cherry tomato that explodes when you stick a fork into it? Comedian Rich Hall calls it a *squigger*. He didn't find the word in the dictionary, though; he made it up. Rich invented a lot of words that he thought ought to be in the dictionary but weren't. Do you know what a *pockalanche* is? That's what happens when you lean over to pick up something that fell out of your pockets and then something else falls out. So you lean over to pick that up, and. . . . You get the picture. And what do you call the last slice of pizza in the box, the one that everyone secretly wants but no one is brave enough to claim? Hall calls it the *pigslice*. Not a bad name, huh?

Can you think of anything in your world that there ought to be a name for but there isn't? Make up your own! Share them with your friends, use them when you write, but most of all let them remind you that every word—whether invented a thousand years ago or yesterday—has a story to tell and is alive with meaning.

Chapter 2

Be a Word Detective:

Using Context Clues

Sometimes famous people will complain that reporters have taken their words "out of context." What do they mean? Well, suppose a reporter asked rock star Lindy Lopper what she thought of people who made illegal copies of her music, and Lindy answered, "I think this is a tremendous problem." Then suppose the reporter wrote, "Lopper says illegal recordings are 'tremendous.'"

The reporter would be quoting an actual word that Lindy used, but because the word was quoted *out of context*—that is, separated from the words around it that gave it a certain meaning—the reporter's quote would give exactly the opposite meaning that Lindy intended. To say something is a "tremendous problem" means that it's a huge, difficult problem. To simply say that something is "tremendous," on the other hand, means that it's wonderful.

You'll also see words taken out of context in the newspaper ads for movies. Suppose movie critic Wrecks Read wrote, "*Rocky XV* is a terrific disappointment," but the ad for the movie quoted him as having said, "Terrific!" Again, the word quoted would give exactly the opposite impression of what the person actually meant.

You can see how misleading words used out of context can be. Many words have more than one meaning—the word *set* has more than 200!—and a word's exact meaning in any given situation depends on the words and sentences around it, its *context*.

Taking a good look at the context in which a word appears can sometimes help you discover new meanings for familiar words, or even to figure out the meaning of a word you don't know at all.

New Meanings for Familiar Words

One way to expand your vocabulary is to learn new meanings for familiar words that can be used in different contexts. Now everybody knows the words *run, scale, strike, check, back, beat, charge, clear, front,* and *free*, right? But how many meanings do you know for each of these words? In other words, how many different contexts can you use them in?

TRY IT: Each group of sentences demonstrates different meanings of the same word. In each group, can you think of at least one *more* sentence that demonstrates a different meaning of that word? Write your sentences down on a spare sheet of paper.

Give yourself 5 points for each sentence you come up with. A score of 50 is average, 75 is excellent, and 100 makes you a Word Master.

My dad is in <u>charge</u> of five people at work.

The soldiers <u>charged</u> up the hill.

That man has been <u>charged</u> with murder.

I stepped on the bathroom <u>scale</u> and hoped for the best.

How would you rate him on a <u>scale</u> of 1 to 10?

Two mountaineers will <u>scale</u> that peak this winter.

Using Context Clues

She likes to <u>run</u> in the park every morning.
Do you know how to <u>run</u> this projector?
I wonder how long that movie will <u>run</u>.

He made his meaning perfectly <u>clear.</u>
How long will it take for the check to <u>clear</u>?
The table was made of <u>clear</u> plastic.

Can you <u>strike</u> out that batter?
It took only three <u>strikes</u> of the hammer to get the
    nail in.
I wonder if they'll <u>strike</u> oil.

We paid the doctor by <u>check</u>.
Ask the waiter for our <u>check</u>.
<u>Check</u> off the items you want to order.

I <u>beat</u> the egg whites in a bowl.
This song has a good <u>beat</u>.
The police officer was walking his <u>beat</u>.

They sat in the <u>back</u> of the theater.
Put some suntan lotion on my <u>back</u>.
Who are you <u>backing</u> in the election?

Was that <u>free</u> or did you buy it?
Americans live in a <u>free</u> society.
They drink caffeine-<u>free</u> colas.

She put up a brave <u>front</u>, but I knew she was
    worried.

There's an amazing picture in the <u>front</u> of this
   book.
My grandfather fought on the European <u>front</u>
   during World War II.

How did you do? The moral of the story is to look out
for those old familiar words you think you know. They
can surprise you. Watch how familiar words are used in
your reading, and learn as many meanings for them as
you can. That's one way to expand your understanding of
English without learning a single new word!

The Secret Life of Words
You Learn in School

Believe it or not, some of the special terms you learn in
science or math or English can actually be useful in real
life. All you have to do is put them in a new context.

In health class, for example, you've probably studied
the *knee-jerk* reflex. That's what happens when the doctor
hits your knee with a little rubber hammer and your lower
leg automatically kicks forward a little. How, you might
wonder, could this term ever possibly be useful in any
other context or situation? Well, suppose someone said,
"Don't make such a *knee-jerk* response to all my ideas. At
least stop and think them over before you turn them
down." What does the person mean? In effect, he or she is
comparing the way your brain works to a *knee-jerk* reflex.
The person means that you react automatically, without
thinking. *Knee-jerk response* turns out to be a very de-
scriptive term to apply to certain real-life situations.

How about the term *cliché*? You've probably learned in
English class that expressions such as "good as gold" and
"as busy as a bee" are called clichés. They're overused,

boring, unoriginal ways to express an idea. How might you apply this word in the context of a real-life situation? Well, suppose you saw a new movie with an outer space theme and it reminded you of every other space movie you'd ever seen. You might say, "That movie was full of *clichés*. It didn't have any new ideas or special effects." Instead of using the word *cliché* to talk about words, you'd be using it in a different context, to talk about movies.

Here are some other words from textbooks that can also be applied to real life. How many do you know the meaning of? How could they be applied to real-life situations? Check your dictionary if you're curious.

> inertia
> placebo
> amphibian
> amphibious
> proportion
> variable
> personification
> irony

Using Context Clues to Learn New Words

Here is part of the opening paragraph from the novel *The War of the Worlds* by H. G. Wells:

> No one would have believed in the last years of the nineteenth century that this world was being watched keenly and closely by intelligences greater than man's . . . that as men busied themselves about their various concerns they were *scrutinized* and studied, perhaps almost as narrowly as a man with a microscope might *scrutinize* the . . . creatures that swarm and multiply in a drop of water.

If you didn't already know the meaning of the word *scrutinize* before you read this passage, you probably know its meaning now. *Scrutinize* means to watch or examine something in order to discover the smallest details. The context in which the word appears makes its meaning clear.

What clues did the author give the word's meaning? He included synonyms, words that have nearly the same meaning as *scrutinize*, within the passage. These synonyms include *watched* and *studied*. In fact, the phrase "watched keenly and closely" could actually be used as a definition of *scrutinized*.

Now try reading this passage from *Romeo and Juliet*:

JULIET: O, swear not by the moon, th' *inconstant* moon,
That monthly changes in her circled orb,
Lest that thy love prove likewise variable.

—Act I, Scene 2

Juliet is talking to Romeo, but what is she saying? Can you tell what *inconstant* means from the context in which it is used? Are there any clue words around it? Take another look. Do you think it means *loyal*? *changeable*? *beautiful*? It means *changeable*. What Juliet is asking is for Romeo not to be fickle and fall in love with someone else. Again, there are clues in the passage that tip you off to the meaning of *inconstant*. The words *changes* and *variable* are very close in meaning to the word *inconstant* and can help you figure out the word's meaning. (If you know that the prefix *in* means *not*, you have another clue to the word's meaning. Prefixes and suffixes are discussed in the next chapter.)

Synonyms or definitions are a very common type of context clue. Looking around for such clues when you come across an unfamiliar word in your reading can be a big help. Can you spot the context clues in the following passage from *A Christmas Carol* by Charles Dickens?

> • • •
> "When I use a word," Humpty Dumpty said, "it means just what I choose it to mean—neither more nor less."
> —Lewis Carroll
> • • •

> Again the *specter* raised a cry, and shook his chain and wrung his shadowy hands.
>   "You are *fettered*," said Scrooge trembling. "Tell me why."
>   "I wear the chain I *forged* in life," replied the Ghost. "I made it link by link, and yard by yard."

If you are unfamiliar with the words *specter*, *fettered*, and *forged*, you can find clues to their meanings within the passage. For each word, there is a synonym or definition given as a clue to the word's meaning. Did you spot the clues?

First of all, a specter is a ghost. You can tell that, because the specter who shakes his chain is later referred to as a ghost when he begins to speak.

Fettered means chained. You can tell this because when Scrooge asks the ghost why he is fettered, the ghost explains why he wears a chain. The word *forged*, in this context at least, means to make something out of metal. The ghost says that he *forged* the chain and then defines the word by explaining that he "made" the chain "link by link, and yard by yard."

How did you do? Are you beginning to get the hang of context clues? Well, synonyms and definitions aren't the only kinds of help a writer may give you, so read on about other kinds of context clues.

Sometimes a writer will give you a hint to a word's meaning by contrasting it to a word or idea that means the opposite. For example, here's another passage from *The War of the Worlds* (in this one, the Martians have stopped scrutinizing the earth and are about to take it over!):

> And this was no disciplined march; it was a *stampede*—a stampede gigantic and terrible—without order and without a goal.

In this passage, the author lets you know what a stampede is by telling you what a stampede is NOT. It is NOT a disciplined, orderly march; it is the opposite. A stampede is a sudden rush of people or animals running away from something, as the author explains, "without order and without a goal."

Here's another passage, from the same book, in which you can guess the meaning of a word by its opposite:

> As I watched, the planet seemed to grow larger and smaller and to advance and *recede*, but that was simply that my eye was tired.

You know that *larger* and *smaller* are opposites, so chances are that *advance* and *recede* are, too. And if *advance* means to move forward, then *recede* means . . . to move back, right? Congratulations, you have just taught yourself the meaning of the word *recede*. Of course, you may already have known the word from another context, especially if you happen to know a man who is worried about his *receding* hairline.

What other context clues can you find in your reading? Sometimes authors use *examples* that show what a word means. For example, here's how H. G. Wells describes the *anatomy* of a Martian:

> The internal *anatomy* . . . was almost equally simple. The greater part of the structure was the brain, sending enormous nerves to the eyes, ear, and . . . tentacles. Besides this were the bulky lungs, into which the mouth opened, and the heart and its vessels. . . . And this was the sum of the Martian organs.

First of all, Wells gives us the word *structure* as a clue to the meaning of *anatomy*. He says he's going to talk about the creature's anatomy, and then he goes on to describe its structure. Then he gives us examples of what he's talking about: the brain, the nerves, the eyes, the ears, the tentacles, the lungs, the mouth, the heart. Then he ends up by giving us the clue word *organs*. So we can safely conclude that the anatomy of a creature is its physical structure, its parts, its organs.

Another type of context clue is called a common-sense clue. Here's an example of one from *The Invisible Man*, also by H. G. Wells:

> He was hit hard under the ear, and went reeling, trying to face round towards his unseen *antagonist*.

What is an antagonist? Well, if you'd just been hit from behind, who would you be turning around to face? Your attacker or opponent, the person who had hit you, of course. An antagonist is an opponent.

Here's another passage with a common-sense clue. This one's from *The War of the Worlds*, again. It's a scene that takes place when the hero and another man are trapped in a house surrounded by Martians and are running out of food. See if you can guess the meaning of the word *rations* from the context clues the writer gives:

> In the end I planted myself between him and the food, and told him of my determination to begin a discipline. I divided the food in the pantry into *rations* to last us ten days. I would not let him eat any more that day.

What are rations? Well, simply by reading what the man did with the food, you get a pretty good idea. He divided up the food so that it would last ten days, and decided how much he and the other man could eat each day. Rations are fixed amounts or shares of something. Items are rationed when they are in short supply.

Take the Next Step

The first step in using context clues is to pay attention when you read so you won't miss them. The second step is to take the new words with you after you close the book. You've learned nine new words in this chapter. How many do you remember? Test yourself by answering the following questions:

1. Can you *scrutinize* your watch?
2. Would you want your boyfriend or girlfriend to be *inconstant*?
3. Can having too many problems make people feel as if they are *fettered*?
4. Does a blacksmith *forge* things?
5. Would you want your *antagonist* to *ration* your food?
6. When the ocean *recedes*, is it high tide or low tide?

7. What part of your *anatomy* has been compared to a computer?
8. Would you enjoy standing in the middle of a *stampede*?

Other Word Clues

Context clues can be a wonderful help in figuring out the meanings of unfamiliar words—as long as you can find them, that is. However, writers don't always leave such wonderful clues around for you to find, as you may have noticed. Luckily, though, you have another secret weapon, because the meanings of many words are locked up right inside the words themselves. And all you need are the keys. The keys to unlocking the meanings of many words are prefixes, suffixes, and roots, which you'll learn about in Chapter 3.

Chapter 3

Recognizing Family Resemblances:

Roots, Prefixes, and Suffixes

Words belong to families. Many words share a family resemblance to each other and share the same family history. And, just like with human families, once you get to know one member of the family, it's easier to recognize and get to know the other members.

You may or may not like the fact that you resemble other people in your family, but when it comes to vocabulary study, you should be grateful for family resemblances. They make it much easier to learn new words, because you don't have to learn words one at a time. Every time you learn one word, you're learning a whole family of related words.

Read the words in the following word family. Can you tell what each member of the family has in common?

import
export
portable
transport
transportation
report
reporter

As you probably noticed, each word in the family contains the letters PORT. Each also has something to do with carrying. To *import* means to "carry" goods "in" to a country. To *export* means to "carry" goods "out" of a country. Something *portable* is "able to be carried." To *transport* something is to "carry" it "across" a certain distance. *Transportation* is the "act of carrying" something "across" a certain distance. A *report* is news "carried back" from one place to another. And a *reporter* is the "one who carries back" the news.

PORT is called the *root* of each of the words in this family. It comes from the Latin word *portare*, meaning "to carry." PORT is called a root because it is the most basic part of each word in the family, the part that supplies each word's central meaning.

To expand the meaning of the root PORT, letters were added before and after it. The letters added before the root (*im-*, *ex-*, *trans-*, and *re-*) are called *prefixes*. The letters added after the root (*-able*, *-ation*, and *-er)* are called *suffixes*. Word families are built from roots, prefixes, and suffixes.

Here is another word family you're probably already familiar with, but you may not have thought about how all the words are related. Can you tell the root of each word and figure out the basic meaning it gives to each word?

pendant	independent
pendulum	independence
pending	suspend
depend	suspense
dependent	suspension

The root of each word is PEND, which means "to hang." A *pendant* is something you hang around your neck. A *pendulum* is the swinging piece that hangs from some old-fashioned clocks. To leave someone in *suspense* is to leave them hanging. To *depend* on someone is to "hang" on them. To be *independent* means NOT to "hang "on anyone else. And so on.

TRY IT: Now that you're catching on to word families, see if you can spot the "family resemblances" in the following words. In each group of words, identify the root. Then decide what all the words in the group have in common and choose the word in the list below that best sums up what each root means.

1. The words *autograph, biography,* and *telegraph* all have something to do with _____.
2. The words *telephone, microphone,* and *saxophone* all have something to do with _____.
3. The words *sympathy, pathetic,* and *apathy* all have something to do with _____.
4. The words *biology, geology,* and *psychology* all have something to do with _____.
5. The words *vision, television,* and *visible* all have something to do with _____.

   A. feelings   B. sound   C. writing
   D. seeing   E. science

So far in this chapter, you've already learned seven important roots and some of the members of their word families. If you'd like to continue learning words this way, study the following chart of commonly used roots.

Common Roots and Word Families

Root	Meaning	Examples
bene	good	*bene*fit, *bene*ficial, *bene*factor
chron	time	*chron*ic, *chron*ological, syn*chron*ize
civ	citizen	*civ*ic, *civ*il, *civ*ilian, *civ*ilization
cred	believe	*cred*it, *cred*ible, in*cred*ible, dis*cred*it
dic	say	*dic*tion, pre*dic*t, pre*dic*tion, contra*dic*t, ver*dic*t
duc	lead	in*duc*e, pro*duc*e, re*duc*tion, con*duc*tor, e*duc*ate
dyna	power	*dyna*mite, *dyna*mic, *dyna*mo, *dyna*sty
fin	end, boundary	*fin*ite, *fin*ish, de*fin*e, de*fin*ite, de*fin*ition, in*fin*ity
graph, gram	write	bio*graph*y, auto*graph*, tele*gram*
grat	please, thank	con*grat*ulate, *grat*itude, *grat*eful, *grat*ifying
ject	throw	pro*ject*or, pro*ject*ile, e*ject*, in*ject*ion, re*ject*, de*ject*ed
log	speech, science	mono*log*ue, dia*log*ue, bio*log*y, geo*log*y, psycho*log*y
man	hand	*man*ual, *man*uscript
mit, mis	send, allow	*mis*sile, ad*mit*, per*mit*, pro*mis*e, trans*mis*sion, per*mis*sion
mot, mov, mob	move	*mob*ile, *mot*ion, im*mob*ilize, auto*mob*ile, *mob*ility, *mov*ement

Roots, Prefixes, and Suffixes

Root	Meaning	Examples
onym	name	pseudo*nym*, syno*nym*, an-to*nym*, homo*nym*, anony-mous
pac	peace	*pac*ify, *pac*ifier, *pac*ifist, *Pac*ific
path	feeling	sym*path*y, em*path*y, apa-thy, *path*os
pel, puls	push, drive, force	pro*pel*, ex*pel*, re*pel*, pro*pel*-ler, dis*pel*, pro*puls*ion, com*puls*ion
pend, pens	hang	*pend*ant, *pend*ulum, *pend*-ing, sus*pend*, sus*pens*e, inde*pend*ent
phon	sound	tele*phon*e, micro*phon*e, saxo*phon*e
pos	place	im*pos*e, de*pos*it, *pos*ition, pro*pos*e, trans*pos*e, super-im*pos*e, de*pos*e
prim	first	*prim*ary, *prim*itive, *prim*ate
scop	to watch	tele*scop*e, micro*scop*e, per-i*scop*e
scrip	write	*scrip*t, *scrip*ture, in*scrip*tion
sol	alone	*sol*e, *sol*itary, *sol*o, *sol*iloquy, *sol*itude
tele	distant	*tele*phone, *tele*vision, *tele*-gram
spec	to look	in*spec*t, ex*spec*t, intro*spec*tive, retro*spec*tive, *spec*tator, *spec*imen, *spec*tacular, pro*spec*t
the	god	*the*ology, mono*the*ism, a*the*ism
vert, vers	turn	con*vert*, con*vert*ible, re*vert*, ad*vert*ise, ad*vers*ary

Root	Meaning	Examples
vis, vid	see	*vis*ual, tele*vis*ion, *vis*ible, *vid*eo, *vis*ion, re*vis*e, in*vis*ible
voc, vok	call	pro*vok*e, pro*voc*ative, in*vok*e, e*vok*e, e*voc*ative, in*voc*ation

Prefixes and Suffixes:
The Word Transformers

Being able to use prefixes and suffixes is even more important than knowing about roots. That's because words are kind of like those toys that you can change from one thing to another with a few quick adjustments. You can *transform* the meaning of a word by knowing how to play around with it, by knowing how to add parts to the beginning or the end of the word. Knowing how to play around with words gives you power over them and makes you a word master.

Say you know some people who always *pretend* to be more important than they really are. By knowing about suffixes, you can transform the verb *pretend* to the adjective *pretentious*, and use that word to bring the pretenders back down to earth. Or say you know people who don't act very grown-up or mature for their age. If you know about prefixes, you'll be ready with an adjective that means the opposite of *mature*: *immature*. Someone who always wants to *compete* with you can be described as *competitive*, just by adding a suffix.

Of course, not every prefix and suffix will provide with you a ready-made insult for the people who bug you, but getting to know these handy "word transformers" will help you make sure you're never at a loss for words. Prefixes, you'll discover, can be used to add to or change the meaning of a word. And suffixes can be used to change a word from one part of speech to another—from a noun into an adjective, for example, or from an adjective to a verb.

Refresh Your Memory: Parts of Speech

A *noun* names a person, place, thing, quality, or idea.
EXAMPLE: You have so much *energy*!

A *verb* expresses action or state of being.
EXAMPLE: Your enthusiasm *energizes* the whole class.

An *adjective* describes a person, place, or thing.
EXAMPLES: a. Jane is so *energetic*. b. The *energetic* child wore us all out.

An *adverb* tells how, when, why, where, or to what extent.
EXAMPLE: She works so *energetically*.

Nouns, verbs, adjectives, and adverbs are the four parts of speech that can be transformed by suffixes. The other four parts of speech are the following:

A *pronoun* takes the place of a noun.
EXAMPLES: a. *Rosemary* fixed *Jack's* watch. (nouns) b. *She* fixed *his* watch. (pronouns)

A *conjunction* connects words or groups of words.
EXAMPLES: a. I ordered a burger, some fries, *and* a milkshake. b. Call me tonight *or* tomorrow.

A *preposition* shows the relationship between the noun or pronoun that follows it and some other word in the sentence.
EXAMPLE: The cat is *in* the hat.

An *interjection* expresses strong feeling.
EXAMPLES: a. *Wow*! What a car! b. *Oh, no*! That's my last dollar!

Becoming a Word Master

Study the charts or prefixes and suffixes in this chapter and learn their meanings. Learn as many words as you can from the same word family. You can do this in two ways. First of all, whenever you look up a word in the dictionary, take a quick peek at any related words listed nearby and make them a part of your vocabulary, too. For example, look how many words are derived from the simple word *act*:

act	activity	actively
actor	inactivity	activation
acting	activate	actual
action	inactivate	actuality
inaction	activism	actually
active	activist	actualize
inactive	activator	actualization

Another way to become aware of word families is to look for familiar word parts in unfamiliar words. This system won't always work, because some words look related but really aren't. (The words *putty* and *putrid*, for example, are totally unrelated.) However, the more experience you acquire with word families, the easier it will be for you to tell the true "relatives" from the "impostors." And you can always check your hunches by looking the words up in the dictionary, as you'll learn in the next chapter.

Word Transformers: Prefixes

Prefix	Meaning	Examples
a-	not, without	atypical, apathy, anonymous
a-	on	aboard, ashore
ante-	before	antecedent, antedate, antebellum
anti-	against	antifreeze, antipathy, antibiotic, antidote
auto-	self	autograph, autobiography, autonomy
bi-	two	bicycle, bilateral, bisect
circum-	around	circumference, circumnavigate
co-, com-, con-	together, with	converge, compare, coherent, cohesive
contra-, contro-	against	contradict, controversy
de-	down, away, reverse	descend, depart, defrost
dis-	take away	discourage, discredit, discover
e-, ex-	out	eject, exit, exhale
fore-	before, front	forehead, forearm, foreshadow
il-, im-, in-, ir-	not	illegal, immobile, inactive, irresponsible
inter-	between	intervene, international, intermediate

Prefix	Meaning	Examples
mal-	bad, ill	malfunction, maladjusted
mis-	wrong	misinform, misstatement
mono-	one	monologue, monotheism
neo-	new	neolithic, neoclassical
non-	not	nonprofit, nonviolent, nontoxic
pan-	all	panorama, Pan-American
per-	through	perspire, pervade
peri-	around	perimeter, periscope, peripheral
poly-	many	polygon, polynomial, polysyllabic
post-	after	postscript, postwar, posterity
pre-	before	prejudice, premonition, precede
pro-	forward	protrude, propose, project, propel
re-	back, again	repay, replace, repeat, replay
retro-	back	retroactive, retrospect, retrogress
semi-	half, partly	semicircle, semiprofessional, semiprivate

Prefix	Meaning	Examples
sub-	under	substandard, submarine, subnormal
super-	above, on, over	superimpose, Superman, superpower, superstar, supersonic
sym-, syn-, syl-	together, with	sympathy, synthesis, syllable
trans-	across	transcontinental, transportation
tri-	three	triangle, tricycle, tripod
un-	not	unimportant, unpleasant, unpopular
uni-	one	unity, unify, universal, uniform

Word Transformers: Suffixes

Suffixes	Meaning	Examples	Use
-fy, -ate, -ize, -en	to make, form into	energ*ize*, beauti*fy*, activ*ate*, fresh*en*	to form VERBS
-ly	in a certain manner	quick*ly*, dangerous-*ly*, obvi-ous*ly*	to form ADVERBS
-able, -ible	capable of being, able to, tending to	converti-*ble*, re-mov*able*	to form ADJECTIVES

Suffixes	Meaning	Examples	Use
-al, -ic, -ical	pertaining to	norm*al*, trag*ic*, his-tor*ical*	to form ADJECTIVES
-en, -ish, -y	like or typical of	wood*en*, styl*ish*, satin*y*	to form ADJECTIVES
-ful, -eous, -ious, -ous	full of	beauti*ful*, gas*eous*, env*ious*, fam*ous*	to form ADJECTIVES
-ive	relating to, tending to	creat*ive*, competi-*tive*	to form ADJECTIVES
-er, -or, -ist, -eer, -ant, -ee	one who	sell*er*, typ*ist*, visit*or*, ass*ist*ant, auction*eer*, employ*er*, employ*ee*	to form NOUNS
-ance, -ence, -ity, -ty, -ness, -ship, -dom, -tude	state or quality of	im-port*ance*, differ*ence*, necess*ity*, certain*ty*, sudden-*ness*, friend*ship*, free*dom*, soli*tude*	to form NOUNS
-hood, -ism	condition or quality	mother-*hood*, pat-riot*ism*	to form NOUNS

Suffixes	Meaning	Examples	Use
-age, -ion, -ation, -sion	condition or act of	patron*age*, educat*ion*, imagina-*tion*, per-sua*sion*	to form NOUNS

Playing Around with Prefixes
TRY IT:

1. A <u>premeditated</u> crime is one that the criminal thinks about_____ he or she does it.
2. A <u>biped</u> is a creature that walks on _____ legs.
3. To <u>exhale</u> means to breath _____.
4. An <u>anti-drug</u> campaign is one launched _____ drugs.
5. An <u>intermission</u> is a break that comes _____ two parts of a performance.
6. <u>Automation</u> refers to the use of machines that run _____.
7. The <u>circumference</u> of a circle is the distance _____.
8. To <u>contradict</u> someone is to speak _____ what they say.
9. A <u>transcontinental</u> railroad is one that goes _____ a whole continent.
10. A <u>misadventure</u> is an adventure that goes _____.
11. A <u>polygon</u> is a figure with _____ sides.
12. A <u>postscript</u> is a message added _____ a letter.

13. A <u>subterranean</u> passage is one that goes
_____ the earth.

14. Two lines that <u>converge</u> come _____.

15. A <u>monologue</u> is spoken by _____ person(s).

Transforming Words with Suffixes

TRY IT: Did you know that you could change a verb into a noun? An adjective into a verb? A noun into an adjective? It's easy. All it takes is a few suffixes. TRY IT yourself.

1. The verb that means "to make something <u>electric</u>" is
_____.

2. The verb that means "to act in a <u>social</u> way" is
_____.

3. The noun that means "one who <u>supervises</u>" is
_____.

4. The noun that means a group of people <u>organized</u> for some purpose is _____.

5. An adjective that describes someone who tends to get <u>irritated</u> is _____.

Chapter 4

Look It Up:

Using the Dictionary

A good up-to-date dictionary is your best source of information about words. You probably use a dictionary most often to look up definitions, but it can tell you so much more—*if* you know how to use it.

Let's begin by looking at dictionaries in book form. Although there are online resources and apps available to help you find word meanings, choose the word you need, or help with spelling and pronunciation, it's always a good idea to know how to use a traditional dictionary in book form. We'll look specifically at electronic options later in this chapter.

Types of Dictionaries

First of all, you should know that not all dictionaries are alike. The huge old dictionary you see resting on a stand in many libraries is an *unabridged* dictionary, such as *Merriam Webster's Third New International Dictionary, Unabridged.* Unabridged dictionaries contain the most words—*Webster's Third* has 472,000 entries—but they tend to be out-of-date. Language changes rapidly, and new words seem to be added to our vocabulary by the minute! Commonly used words such as *clone*, *gridlock*, or *videotape* will not be found in a dictionary published before 1970. It would not be the best place to look up a new meaning of an old word, either, or check whether a compound word such as *videotape* should be spelled as one word or two. The spelling of a compound—whether it is hyphenated, written as one word, or written as two—changes over time as the word becomes more familiar. You need to consult an up-to-date dictionary to find out the most current spelling, pronunciation, and usage of words. Unabridged dictionaries are useful for looking up technical terms you won't find in other dictionaries, or for looking up a rarely used meaning of a common word.

The best dictionaries for students are referred to as *college, school and office*, or *desk* dictionaries. Good ones include *Merriam-Webster's Collegiate Dictionary*, Eleventh Edition, *Webster's New World Dictionary: Second College Edition*, *The Random House Dictionary*, and the *American Heritage Dictionary of the English Language*.

A college or desk dictionary is about the size of a textbook. It is small enough to be carried from room to room, but you probably wouldn't want to haul one around in your backpack. A college dictionary contains fewer entries than an unabridged dictionary, but it is more up-to-date. If you are serious about words, or plan to go to college, you should own one of these dictionaries. Until you can afford one, you can consult the college dictionaries in your school library or local public library. Like an unabridged dictionary, a college dictionary tells much more than a word's definition. That's why it is more useful than a *pocket dictionary*. A college dictionary gives a brief history of each entry word, lists more definitions and synonyms, and gives more detailed explanations than a pocket dictionary does. It labels words that are considered slang, and lists more related forms of a word than a pocket dictionary can. Pocket dictionaries are useful mostly for checking spelling and pronunciation, and for looking up definitions of common words.

Using the Dictionary:
Alphabetical Order and Guide Words

Dictionary entries are arranged in *alphabetical order*. Words beginning with *a* are listed first, then words beginning with *b*, *c*, *d*, and so on all the way to *z*. Words that begin with the same first letter are arranged according to the second letter of each word. That means that a word beginning with *ab* would come before a word beginning with *ac*. A word beginning with *ac* would come before a word beginning *ad*, which would come before *af*, and so on.

Words that have the same first two letters are arranged according to their third letters. That means that a word beginning with *aba* would come before a word beginning with *abb* or *abd*. Words with the same first three letters are arranged according to their fourth letters, and so on.

This system makes sense, but it can still take a long time to find the word you want—unless you've discovered *guide words*. By becoming a whiz at guide words, you can spend a lot less time looking up words in the dictionary. Here's how they work:

On every page of a dictionary, there is one word printed in heavy type at the top of the left-hand column, and one printed in heavy type at the top of the right-hand column. These guide words are like boundary lines. The word over the left column tells you the first entry on that page, and the word over the right column tells you the last entry on that page. Every word defined on that page must come alphabetically *between* the two guide words.

Say that you want to look up the word *huggermugger*, for example (A real word, honest! Look it up!). You drag out your dictionary and it falls open to a page with the guidewords *Chihuahua* and *chimney sweep*. Obviously, you've got a ways to go, because you're only in the *c*'s and you need to be in the *h*'s. So you flip through pages until you see one with the guide words *heartache* and *heathen*. Well, now you're getting warmer. At least you're in the *h*'s. But both those words start with *he* and you want a word that starts with *hu*. You flip some more pages until you get to the guide words *horsefeathers* and *hospitalization insurance*. Now you're pretty warm, because *o* is the vowel that comes right before the vowel *u*, so it's time to start turning the pages more slowly. Let's see, there's *hotspur* and *housekeeper*. No. *Housekeeping* and *howling monkey*? Close, but no cigar. *Howrah* and *huh*? Success! The word you want starts with *hug*. Since *huh* is on that page, *huggermugger* must be, too, because *hug* comes before *huh* and after *how*.

Spelling and Syllable Division

Now that you've found *huggermugger*, what do you see? Here's what you'd find in *Webster's New World Dictionary, Second College Edition* (Simon & Schuster, 1982):

> **hug•ger•mug•ger** (hug′ ər mug′ ər) *n.* [earlier also *hokermoker*, apparently rhyming compound based on ME. *Mokeren*, to hoard, conceal, whence the basic sense "secrecy"] 1. A confusion; muddle; jumble 2. [Archaic] secrecy — *adj.* 1. confused; muddled; jumbled 2. [Archaic] secret — *adv.* 1. In a confused or jumbled manner 2. [Archaic] secretly — *vt.* To keep secret — *vi.* To behave in a secretive or confused way.

First of all, you find out how to spell the word. The fact that there's a dot between the *hugger* and the *mugger* tells you that the two parts should be written together as one word. If there was a blank space between the two parts, that would mean that they should be written as two separate words.

Next, you see that the word has four syllables: hug·ger·mug·ger. These syllable divisions show you places where you could break the word at the end of a line of writing or typing if you didn't have room to write the whole word on one line.

Pronunciation

Then, in parentheses, you see the pronunciation of the word: (hug′ ər mug′ ər). Luckily, it's pronounced just the way you might expect. The *hug* part sounds exactly like the word *hug*, and the *mug* part sounds exactly like the word *mug*.

It's very important to understand the system your dictionary uses to show how to pronounce words, so that you can look up words and figure out how to pronounce them on your own. If you can't pronounce a word, you're not likely to use it much, right?

Here's the system my dictionary uses to indicate vowel sounds. Your dictionary probably uses a similar one:

> *a* (sometimes shown as ă) means the sound of *a* in *apple.*
> ā means the sound of *a* in *cake.*
> ä means the sound of *a* in *car.*
> *e* (sometimes shown as ĕ) means the sound of *e* in *red.*
> ē means the sound of *e* in *equal.*
> *i* (sometimes shown as ĭ) means the sound of *i* in *hit.*
> ī means the sound of *i* in *bike.*
> ō means the sound of *o* in *bone.*
> ôr means the sound of *o* in *corn.*

$\overline{oo}$ means the sound of *oo* in *school*.
oo means the sound of *oo* in *book*.
oi means the sound of *oi* in *boil*.
ou means the sound of *ou* in *out*.
u (sometimes shown as ŭ) means the sound of *u* in
    up.
ur means the sound of *ur* in *fur; er herd; or* in *word*.
ə means the "uh" sound in *a*cross, cat*e*gory,
    med*i*cine, *a*lcohol, and foc*u*s.

A dictionary's pronunciation key is usually listed at the front of the dictionary and is often repeated at the bottom of each page.

Go back for a moment to the dictionary entry for *huggermugger*, and notice the two marks that look like slanted apostrophes (hug′ ər mug′ ər). These are *accent marks*. They show you which syllables get the stress or heavy beats. One mark is heavier than the other because it gets a slightly heavier beat. Pronouncing a word is a lot like tapping out a drumbeat. Here's how *huggermugger* would look if you tapped it out (the larger the type, the heavier the beat):

HUG er MUG er

Parts of Speech

After the pronunciation guide in the *huggermugger* entry, you'll see a small letter *n*. This tells you what part of speech the word is. *Huggermugger* is a noun, a thing. If you glance through the rest of the entry, you'll also see the abbreviations *adj.*, a*dv.*, *vt.*, and *vi*. These tell you that the word can also be an adjective, an adverb, or a verb. Here are the abbreviations used to indicate parts of speech:

n. = noun
pron. = pronoun
v., *vi.*, or *vt.* = verb
adj. = adjective
adv. = adverb
prep. = preposition
conj. = conjunction
interj. = interjection

To review the parts of speech, go back to Chapter 3. You may think that you hear enough about parts of speech in English class. However, it does come in handy to know whether a new word stands for a thing, an action, or a description. Some words can be all three. Think of *end*, *set*, or *wax*.

Word History

The next thing you'll see in the dictionary entry for *huggermugger* are some brackets [   ] with an explanation inside them. This information tells the history of the word, what language it comes from, the root word from that language, and any other interesting facts about the word's history. This part of the entry often contains abbreviations such as *L.* for Latin, *Gr.* for Greek, *Fr.* for French, and so on. The word history for *huggermugger* says that it is based on *ME.*, meaning Middle English, a historical stage in the development of English in England. To find out what all the word history abbreviations mean, check the front of your dictionary. You can often find out some interesting facts in this part of a dictionary entry.

Finally, the Definitions

At last, we've come to the numbered definitions of *huggermugger*. What in the world does it mean? The first definition is "a confusion, muddle, jumble." That means you could say, "I left my room in a *huggermugger* this morning." Or, "I feel as if I'm in such a *huggermugger* today."

The second definition is "secrecy," but it is labeled *[Archaic]*. That means you might find this meaning used in an old book, but the word isn't used that way anymore. Sometimes you'll see definitions that are labeled *[Colloq.]* or *[Sl.]*. These abbreviations stand for *colloquial* and *slang*. They indicate that a word can be appropriately used in some situations, but not in others. You'll find out more about slang in Chapter 6.

When we look through the definitions of *huggermugger* as an adjective, adverb, and verb, we can imagine several different ways of using the word:

adjective: You have such a *huggermugger* brain.
(muddled)
adverb: I can't believe how *huggermugger* they
planned this dance. (in a confused manner)
verb: I expect you to *huggermugger* what I tell you
about Michelle and Danny. (keep secret)
verb: He's *huggermuggering* around as if he were in a
fog. (acting confused)

Note: Sometimes the dictionary will actually list two entirely different entries with different sets of definitions for the same word. For example, if you look up the word *well* you'll find two different entries, labeled *well*[1] and *well*[2]. Under *well*[1] you'll find the definitions that have to do with a hole in the ground dug for water. Under *well*[2] you'll find the definitions that have to do with how a person does something or how a person feels. The two sets of meanings are listed separately because they are totally unrelated. Be on the lookout for these separate entries when you look up an unfamiliar word. If you overlook one, you could end up really confused.

Synonyms

A good dictionary will also list any synonyms (words that have nearly the same meaning) of the entry word. It may even explain how the synonyms are alike in meaning, and in what ways they are different. You'll learn more about synonyms in Chapter 5.

Related Words and Phrases

Your dictionary may list related words and phrases at the end of an entry. At the end of the entry for *ground*, for example, you may find definitions of the phrases *get off the ground*, *hold one's ground*, *lose ground*, *on firm ground*, and *run into the ground*. At the end of the entry for *acceptable* are listed the words *acceptability*, *acceptableness*, and *acceptably*. They are not defined because if you know the meaning of *acceptable*, then you can figure out the meanings of these words, too. They are listed just so you'll know that they exist and how they're spelled.

Irregular Forms

If the plural of a noun is not formed in the usual way (by adding *s* or *es*), the plural will be listed at the beginning of the entry, after the abbreviation *pl.* (*geese*, for example). If the past and past participle of a verb are formed in an irregular way (instead of simply adding *d* or *ed*), these forms will be listed at the beginning of the verb entry (*began*, *begun*). If an adjective or adverb forms its comparative and superlative forms in an irregular way, these will be listed at the beginning of the entry. (Remember, the *comparative* form is used to compare two items: that joke is *sillier* than the one you told yesterday. The *superlative* is used to compare three or more: That is the *silliest* joke I've ever heard.) For example, the forms *better* and *best* are listed at the beginning of the entry for *good*.

And That's Not All

Your dictionary may include helpful charts, tables, and illustrations. It may feature separate alphabetized glossaries of people and places, or of foreign expressions used in English. These are usually located at the back of the dictionary. There may also be a guide to grammar and punctuation in your dictionary, as well as other kinds of useful information. Know what your dictionary can do for you and practice using it. Most of all, remember to pick it up off the shelf, dust it off, and *use it* when you're stuck for some little bit of information. You never know when it might come in handy.

Online and Electronic Dictionaries

There are plenty of dictionaries and other resources about words and language available online and in other electronic formats, including ones that can be used on cell phones and other portable devices. A good example is the web site www.dictionary.com. These resources provide everything that a good dictionary in book form can offer, and sometimes much more.

For example, some online dictionaries provide a link through which you can hear the word pronounced. They also provide links to other web sites that give more detailed information about the origin and history of the word. They can connect you quickly to synonyms and antonyms and other related words and present you with more choices for your writing and speech.

Unlike dictionaries in book form, electronic dictionaries do not need to utilize guide words, but they are more difficult to browse through than books—and browsing a dictionary can be a surprisingly entertaining activity. Whether your main dictionary is electronic or print, it's good to grasp the fundamentals of using both types—from guide words to pronunciation symbols to abbreviations—so that wherever you are you can find the words you need to communicate most effectively.

1. **TRY IT**: Suppose a page in your dictionary has the guide words *toothpick* and *topminnow*. Which of the following words would appear on that page?

toothpaste	topaz	top hat	topic sentence	top
toothsome	torpedo	top-heavy	tourist	tonsil
top banana	traffic	topnotch	toast	

2. Here are the pronunciations of some very common words. Can you figure out what they are?

kāk _____
wim′ in _____
thur′ ō _____
nā′ bər _____
siks _____
ə noi′ _____
hit _____
hīt _____

3. How many parts of speech can the following words be? Can you use each one in all its different meanings?

a. toy   f. welcome
b. run   g. ground
c. program   h. fast
d. produce   i. ready
e. well

Chapter 5

In Other Words . . .

Synonyms and Antonyms

Using Words to Organize the World

Human beings love to organize things. Every day our brains take in thousands of bits of information about the world, and try to make sense of it all. In ways that scientists are only just beginning to understand, each human brain operates as an amazing filing system that stores everything a person knows about the world—from fantasy-league batting averages and the words of the latest viral hit song to important dates in American history (if you're lucky).

One of the most basic ways we organize information is by grouping similar ideas together. Think of the way a supermarket is organized. Similar types of products are shelved together. There might be an entire aisle of breakfast cereals, another one of coffee, a section where all the spices can be found, and a whole refrigerator aisle full of dairy products. All of the products in a given section have something in common, yet they are not exactly the same. One cereal may have a different flavor, texture, and nutritional value than another. Milk, cottage cheese, ice cream, and yogurt are all related, but you don't use them in exactly the same way, or in exactly the same situations. (Most people don't like hot fudge sauce on their cottage cheese, for example!) So it is with words.

The English language can be broken down into groups of words that express similar ideas. Within each group, however, few of the words have *exactly* the same meaning or are completely interchangeable. Words with similar meanings are called *synonyms*. Learning about synonyms is one of the most important ways to improve your vocabulary.

Synonyms and the Thesaurus

A *thesaurus* is a dictionary of synonyms. You can think of it as a grocery store of words and ideas, because a thesaurus organizes words the way a grocery store organizes products. By walking through a grocery store, you can get an idea of the general categories of items people buy to take care of their daily needs. Similarly, by glancing through a thesaurus, you will see the general categories people have developed to talk about their experiences. You'll find headings for DANGER, LOVE, MONEY, COWARDICE, SUCCESS, FAILURE, and thousands more, listed in alphabetical order.

Some entries in the thesaurus list only a few synonyms. Others list almost half a page of related ideas. Turning to one of these entries is like turning down an aisle in the supermarket. Suddenly, you're faced with a confusing variety of choices. For example, suppose you were in the market to talk about some SURPRISE in your life. If you turned to the S section of the thesaurus and looked the word up, here's what you'd find (*Roget's College Thesaurus*, NAL, p. 494):

SURPRISE

Nouns — nonexpectation, unexpectedness, the unforeseen, unforeseen contingency, miscalculation, astonishment, wonder, surprise, thunderclap, blow, shock, bolt out of the blue.

Verbs — **1.** not expect, be taken by surprise, miscalculate, not bargain for. **2.** be unexpected, come unawares, turn up, pop up, drop from the clouds, burst, steal, creep up on one, take by surprise, take unawares, catch napping. *Slang*, come from left field. **3.** surprise, astonish, amaze, astound; dumbfound, startle, dazzle; strike with wonder *or* awe; electrify; stun, stagger, strike dumb, stupefy, petrify, confound, bewilder, flabbergast, fascinate, turn the head, take away one's breath; make one's hair stand on end, make one's eyes pop, take by surprise. *Colloq.*, bowl over, knock for a loop.

Adjectives — **1.** surprised, nonexpectant, unsuspecting, unwarned, off one's guard, inattentive. See WONDER. **2.** surprising, unexpected, unlooked for, unforeseen, unhoped for, beyond expectation, unheard of, startling, sudden.

Adverbs — surprisingly, unexpectedly, abruptly, unawares, without warning, like a bolt from the blue, suddenly. *Colloq.*, smack.

    Antonym, see EXPECTATION.

First, you have to decide whether you want a noun, a verb, an adjective, or an adverb, because the words related to *surprise* are arranged on different "shelves" according to their part of speech. Well, suppose what you wanted to say was that something had *surprised* you, but you didn't want to use the word *surprised* because you were tired of it and had decided it was too boring. So what you need is a verb.

Looking at the synonyms for the verb *surprise*, you still find all kinds of choices. How do you know which word to use? Just as when you're choosing a product in the supermarket, the best guide is your own experience or that of a reliable authority. Choose a synonym you've used before, or one you've seen used in print or heard used by a well-informed speaker. If you're not familiar with a particular synonym at all, look it up in the dictionary or ask someone who knows about words. Remember, just as milk and ice cream and cottage cheese are not interchangeable, neither are most synonyms.

To understand why, take another look at the synonyms for *surprise* as a verb. These include:

astound	stagger
astonish	petrify
amaze	bewilder
startle	flabbergast
dazzle	fascinate
electrify	take away one's breath
stun	make one's hair stand on end
dumbfound	make one's eyes pop
stupefy	knock for a loop

From your experience with words, you can probably tell that most of these synonyms do not have exactly the same meaning. Some express different degrees of surprise or different kinds of surprises. For example, you might be *surprised* to get an A in math. You might even be *bewildered* if you had gotten C's on all of your tests that semester. You wouldn't be *petrified* unless you thought it was a mistake and were afraid someone was going to find out. And you wouldn't say you were *startled* unless your report card sneaked up behind you, tapped you on the shoulder, and made you jump.

If the surprise left you speechless, you could say you were *dumbfounded* or *flabbergasted*. If it left you totally unable to function, you might say you were *stunned* or *stupefied*. Even if you were pretty happy about it, though, you probably wouldn't say you were *electrified*. The word *electrified* suggests a shock of excitement, a thrill that most people just do not get from their grades, no matter how good they are.

The moral of the story is that it's fun to go "shopping" for words in a thesaurus, but you can't load up your cart with just any old words. It's important to know the differences between synonyms as well as the similarities.

Synonyms Paint a Picture

Good writers and speakers want to make a strong impression on their audiences. They want to make their audiences experience something in their imaginations. That's why they use vivid words that paint a picture in the listener's or reader's mind, words that will allow someone to see, hear, touch, taste, or smell what the writer or speaker is talking about.

For example, if you said, "I walked home in wet sneakers," you would not create a vivid impression in your listeners' minds. If you said, "I walked home in damp sneakers," your listeners would have a clearer impression of your experience. In this case, they might say, "So? That's not so bad." But what if you said, "I walked home in *soaked*, *soggy* sneakers"? Now your listeners can feel themselves sloshing around in your disgusting shoes. Now they might answer, "Yuck! How gross!" Mission accomplished. You've communicated what happened so that other people can imagine the experience.

For any experience you want to describe, you can choose general, "blah" words that will put your audience to sleep, or vivid, precise words that will put your audience "in your shoes," so to speak, allowing them to share your experience.

For every "blah" word, however, there may be several different synonyms that express quite different shades of meaning. To get your message across, you need to be able to choose synonyms carefully.

Here's another example. Suppose someone said to you, "We walked through the woods yesterday." What image do you have in your mind? Notice how the image changes as you replace the word *walked* with more specific synonyms:

We *hiked* through the woods yesterday.
We *strolled* through the woods yesterday.
We *trudged* through the woods yesterday.
We *marched* through the woods yesterday.
We *scrambled* through the woods yesterday.
We *wandered* through the woods yesterday.
We *tiptoed* through the woods yesterday.
We *sneaked* through the woods yesterday.
We *bushwhacked* through the woods yesterday.

TRY IT: Look at the following sentences. Under each are four words: one general, "blah" word followed by three specific synonyms that create different impressions. Which synonym best completes each sentence? If you're not sure of the words' exact meanings, look them up in the dictionary. When you're finished, you'll have added 15 synonyms to your vocabulary.

1. It's so peaceful to sit on the beach and feel the cool ocean _____ on a hot day. (winds — gales, breezes, blasts)

2. We jumped back quickly as the oil began to _____ out of the ground. (flow — gush, squirt, trickle)
3. It's very inspiring to watch an eagle _____ over the mountain tops. (fly — flutter, flit, soar)
4. There's nothing like the warm, romantic _____ of a big crackling fire in a fireplace. (light — flicker, glow, glare)
5. After I told the joke, his _____ echoed throughout the room and could even be heard across the hall. (laughter — giggles, chuckles, guffaws)

Synonyms Get the Idea Across

As you have seen, by choosing the right synonym, you can make your audience see, hear, feel, smell, or taste something that you have experienced. You can also make sure that you communicate your ideas as clearly as possible.

For example, there are many synonyms for the word *old*, but some of them express different ideas than others. To say that something is *ancient*, for instance, means that it existed long ago, during the early history of civilization. Something *prehistoric* is even older; it dates back to before the time of written records. *Antique* used to mean the same as *ancient*, but we don't use it that way much anymore. Something doesn't have to be very old to be considered antique nowadays—just old enough for people to be willing to pay lots of money for it at an antiques store or flea market.

If you say that something—or someone!—is *decrepit*, you're expressing an additional idea beyond mere oldness. You're saying that it is falling apart or worn out. If you say a thing or idea is *obsolete*, you're saying it's out-of-date. A computer or smartphone doesn't have to be very old to be considered obsolete, does it?

Some synonyms express different degrees of a quality. For example, *rage* and *irritation* are both synonyms for *anger*, but if you were rating degrees of anger from 1 to 10, *irritation* would be at 1 and *rage* would be at 10. The same goes for synonyms of *afraid*. *Nervous* and *apprehensive* would be at one end of the scale, while *terrified*, *petrified*, and *aghast* would be at the other.

You will get your ideas across much more vividly if you use a strong, specific synonym instead of relying on "blah" modifiers such as *very*, *sort of*, and *really*. Instead of saying, "I was really scared," say, "I was *terrified*." Instead of saying, "I was sort of angry," say, "I was *irritated*," if that's what you mean by "sort of angry."

The English language contains a fascinating variety of synonyms that express different shades of meaning for all kinds of ideas. But in order for the words to remain useful, people have to know what they mean. A good college dictionary—whether in print form or online—lists and discusses the distinctions between synonyms at the end of many entries. You might also find it interesting to browse through the *Merriam-Webster Dictionary of Synonyms and Antonyms*, which helps to understand the shades of meaning expressed by many common synonyms.

Synonyms Express Opinions and Attitudes

When we talk and write, we're often interested in more than just sharing facts. Much of the time, we're also expressing an opinion, telling how we feel, and trying to persuade other people to feel the same way. Sometimes we express an opinion simply by choosing one synonym rather than another. That's because words have *connotations* as well as *denotations*.

The *denotation* of a word is its dictionary definition. The *connotations* of a word are the feelings that the word suggests to people. For example, the dictionary definition of *Friday* just says that it's the sixth day of the week. But to many people, the word *Friday* suggests much more than that. When they say, "Thank goodness it's Friday," they mean more than "thank goodness it's the sixth day of the week." When people hear the word *Friday*, they may think of getting out of school or work for the weekend, going out with someone special, staying up late, going away for a short vacation, taking time to do something they really love, watching basketball or football games, seeing someone who's coming to visit for the weekend, and so on. Hearing the word *Friday* can arouse pleasant emotions— relief, hope, excitement, expectation, relaxation, letting go—for many people. These feelings are not included in the dictionary definition, but none of us can separate our feelings about Friday from the word itself. For most people, it's a word with strong positive connotations.

The words *Monday morning*, on the other hand, have negative connotations for many people. Just hearing the words can make them feel tired and depressed. Not everybody attaches the same connotations to every word, however. Connotations can be very personal. The way a word makes us feel depends on our own unique experiences and points of view.

To some people, for example, the word *old-fashioned* has pleasant connotations. They think of the quaint, charming clothes and furniture that they see in old pictures or in movies. When they hear the word *old-fashioned*, they imagine a way of life different from the one we have today, and that seems appealing to them. To other people, the word *old-fashioned* suggests unpleasant connotations—out-of-date ideas that prevent people from appreciating anything that is new and exciting, or from making progress. What the word suggests to you depends on your experiences and your view of the past.

> The difference between the right word and the almost right word is the difference between lightning and the lightning bug.
> —Mark Twain

Some words actually refer to very similar things, but have very different connotations. For example, there is very little difference in the dictionary definitions of *normal, average,* and *mediocre*. They all describe someone or something that is no better or no worse than what is typical. Yet we generally apply these words in different contexts and attach very different feelings to them. Most people want to be considered *normal,* but they would rather not be described as *average.* And to be described as *mediocre* is considered an insult. The feelings we attach to these three words reflect our conflicting attitudes about being no better and no worse than anyone else.

Words with strong connotations can be useful and colorful. Poets use strong connotative words to evoke feelings in us, but words with strong connotations can also be used to manipulate people, to slant the truth. Despite what Shakespeare said about a rose by any other name smelling just as sweet, the name or label we put on something can be important. A person who plants a bomb in a public place may call himself a *freedom fighter,* for example, but most of us would call him a *terrorist.* The two names express totally different opinions of the action.

Words that carry a built-in positive or negative judgment are called "loaded" words. Politicians and advertisers are often guilty of using loaded words to manipulate people's opinions. Advertisers, for example, know that words such as *natural* and *imported* cause many people to respond positively to a product, without ever stopping to think about what the words really mean. People often don't realize that they're responding more to a word than to whether a product actually has anything to offer them.

TRY IT: How aware are you of the connotations of words? Identify the word in each pair that has negative connotations.

1. crowd, mob
2. trusting, gullible
3. abandon, leave
4. confrontation, meeting
5. foolhardy, brave
6. doctor, quack
7. dark, gloomy
8. pushy, aggressive
9. discussion, argument
10. proud, arrogant
11. thrifty, stingy
12. scheme, plan
13. smell, stench
14. underhanded, secret

Synonyms Should Fit the Situation

Sometimes a synonym may express the correct shade of meaning you want to communicate, but will be inappropriate in certain situations. For example, you might tell a friend that you think a certain person or idea is pretty *flaky*, but you shouldn't use that word in a school report, even if it accurately describes what you think of something. That's because *flaky* is a slang term that is relatively new and one that not everyone would understand or appreciate. The words *odd*, *unconventional*, or *eccentric* would be more appropriate in a written report. You'll find out more about what makes language "appropriate," "proper," and "good" in the next chapter.

Antonyms

Suppose someone told you to stop being so *belligerent*. Your answer might well be, "What does that mean?" If the person responded, "Well, you haven't exactly gone out of your way to be friendly and agreeable. In fact, you've done just the opposite," then you would have a good idea of what *belligerent* means. It means the opposite of *friendly* and *agreeable*. It means *unfriendly* and *disagreeable*, in an active way. It's a word used to describe someone who's looking for a fight.

By telling you what *belligerent* was the opposite of, the person gave you a kind of definition of the word. Another word for opposite is *antonym*. Antonyms can be a big help in vocabulary study. If you look up a word in the dictionary and are not sure you understand the definition, look at the end of the entry where synonyms (abbreviated *syn.*) are listed. If you don't recognize any of the synonyms, you may recognize one of the antonyms (listed in the dictionary after the abbreviation *ant.*). And knowing an antonym can be just as useful as knowing a synonym.

For example, if you look up the word *fictitious*, you may find the antonyms *real* and *true* listed at the end of the entry. These tell you that *fictitious* means the opposite of *real* and *true*. It means *imaginary* or *false*.

As you may remember from Chapter 2, writers often use antonyms as context clues. They'll tell you what something is *not*, in order to give you an idea of what it *is*. Not every word has an antonym. There is no such thing as the opposite of *pencil*, for instance; there is no word that means "not a pencil." But much of life is organized according to opposites. As a child, you learned how the world works by mastering the ideas behind such simple antonyms as *high/low*, *good/bad*, *open/closed*, *empty/full*, *hot/cold*, and *happy/sad*. And, as you mature, your mind takes in more complex ideas about the world in terms of opposites. For example, you may learn that some people are described as *optimists* because of their positive outlook on life, while their opposites, *pessimists,* have a negative outlook on life. You may begin contrasting situations that represent *order* with those that represent *chaos* (disorder). And so on.

Antonyms and Standardized Tests

Many standardized tests, such as the Scholastic Aptitude Test (SAT), use antonyms to test your understanding of both vocabulary and the relationships between one idea and another. Antonyms often show up in the *Analogies* section of a test. An analogy tests your understanding of relationships. Here's what one looks like:

BELLIGERENCE : FRIENDLINESS = BLAME : _____
  a. sadness **b**. criticism **c**. praise

If that looks like some kind of secret code to you, you're right. It is. Here's what it means: The symbol : on the left side of the analogy means "is related to." And the equal sign in the middle can be translated as "in the same way that." So what the analogy says is that "*Belligerence* is related to *friendliness* in the same way that *blame* is related to _____." Your job is to choose which of the three choices—*sadness, criticism,* or *praise*—is the correct word to fill in the blank.

You learned above that *belligerence* and *friendliness* are opposites, right? If the two words on the left of an analogy are opposites, then the two words on the right side should be opposites, too. What is the opposite of *blame*? Answer **c**, *praise. Belligerence* is related to *friendliness* in the same way that *blame* is related to *praise*. Each word is paired with its opposite.

Not every problem in an analogies test is based on antonyms, but many are. That's only one reason for learning antonyms. Whenever you learn a new word, test your understanding of the idea it represents by seeing if you can think of an antonym for the word. It's good practice.

Prefixes and Suffixes That Form Antonyms

In Chapter 3, you learned to transform the meanings of words by adding prefixes and suffixes. You can often transform a word into its antonym by adding the correct prefix or suffix. Some prefixes that can be used to form opposites are *un-*, *im-*, *in-*, *ir-*, *il-*, and *dis-*. Here are some examples:

UN-
happy – *un*happy
willing - *un*willing
important – *un*important

IL-
legal – *il*legal
literate – *il*literate
logical – *il*logical

IM-
mature – *im*mature
possible – *im*possible
practical – *im*practical

DIS-
like – *dis*like
belief – *dis*belief
obey – *dis*obey

IN-
visible – *in*visible
expensive – *in*expensive
significant – *in*significant

IR-
regular – *ir*regular
resistible – *ir*resistible
responsible – *ir*responsible

Using these prefixes is one of the important techniques you can use to transform words, but prefixes also cause many people to become confused and make spelling errors. To learn more about using prefixes correctly, see the spelling rules in Chapter 8.

Some prefixes used to form antonyms come in pairs. For example, the opposite of *under*estimate is *over*estimate The opposite of *in*hale is *ex*hale. And so on. Learning to use pairs of prefixes to form antonyms is another skill that can come in handy.

The most common pairs of suffixes used to form antonyms are *–ful* and *–less*. They appear in the common words *useful* and *useless*, *hopeful* and *hopeless*, and many others.

Remember, you can use synonyms and antonyms to communicate your experiences and ideas more clearly, or to express your opinions and attitudes. Knowing a lot of synonyms will help you select the best word for any given situation. And learning synonym-antonym pairs is a good way to help yourself understand how the world of ideas is organized.

Now you're ready to take on one of the trickiest parts of using words. What is "good" English? What determines whether a word is appropriate or inappropriate for a given situation? And why does it matter? These issues are discussed Chapter 6.

Chapter 6

What Is Good English?

Good English Is Clear

So far in this book, you've learned ways to send and receive messages more clearly. You've learned how to use context clues to get at the meaning of words. You've learned to use the dictionary to find out all kinds of information about a word, including its precise definition. You've learned to identify word families and use prefixes and suffixes to transform the meanings of words. You've learned to use synonyms to express different shades of meaning, and you've learned how words can sometimes be defined through their opposites, their antonyms. Learning to use words that mean precisely what you mean to say is an important part of good English, but it is not the only part.

Good English Is Considerate

Good speakers and writers are always aware of their audience. They want to communicate their feelings and ideas to "reach" their audience in some way. So they are careful not to use words and expressions that their readers and listeners might not understand. And they try to express themselves in a way that will not offend their audience or distract the audience's attention away from the message that is being communicated.

Most of us speak and write several different kinds of English, depending on our audience. You probably talk one way with your friends, another way with your parents, and yet another way with your teachers. If you have a little brother or sister, you probably speak a special, simplified language with him or her. And the way you express yourself on paper, in a book report, for example, is probably slightly different from the way you talk. You have different kinds of writing styles, too. If you were writing a funny story, for example, you would use different kinds of words than you would use in a serious report on nuclear war or cancer.

These differences are normal. In fact, people who study the way we use language have classified these differences into four levels of English: *formal, standard, informal,* and *nonstandard.*

Formal English is usually written rather than spoken. It usually contains more "big" words than other kinds of writing, and uses longer, more complicated sentences to express complex ideas. You'll find formal writing in legal documents and scholarly articles and books. Not all formal writing is "good" English. Some people who use this level write in a way that is unnecessarily stiff and hard to understand. Some of the best examples of good formal writing are in the Declaration of Independence and the United States Constitution. Even though these documents contain some "hard" words, they still beautifully express the convictions of their writers even today, more than two hundred years after they were written.

Standard English. If you want to go to college or get a job in a professional or service industry, it's important to be able to speak and write standard English. It is the type of language accepted by and expected of educated people. Standard English is the type of English spoken by newscasters and other television and radio personalities. It is the type of English used by writers in newspapers, magazines, and on web sites intended for a general audience. It's the type of English you should use for a school report or business letter. Standard English is "correct." It obeys all the rules of English grammar that you learn in school. Standard English doesn't use a lot of big words the way formal English does, but it does avoid slang and other informal expressions.

Informal English. This is the type of English you speak with your friends and family. Not everybody speaks the same type of informal English, though. Your informal speech depends on the part of the country you live in, your age, your cultural heritage, the neighborhood you live in, and so on. Informal speech includes slang expressions such as "out to lunch" for crazy, "serious" for good, "later" for good-bye, and "hairy" for nerve wracking. If any of these expressions seem odd to you, then you see the problem with slang. Not everyone uses the same slang expressions, and many slang expressions don't last very long. So if you want your words of wisdom to be appreciated by as many people as possible (or at least by your teacher) for as long as possible (or at least until next week), go easy on the slang. Just imagine what problems we'd have if the Constitution had been written in the slang words of 1789! There'd be nobody around to "translate" it for us.

Nonstandard English. Nonstandard English is "incorrect." It doesn't follow the rules of standard English grammar. Nonstandard English includes such expressions as *ain't*, *anywheres*, *he done*, *she brung*, and so on. It may not seem fair, but people judge you as much by how you say something as by what you say. So, if you want to be accepted in the world where standard English is important, learn it and use it when you need to.

The following examples show how the same idea might be expressed on different language levels:

FORMAL: Pardon me, I was wondering if you might be so kind as to indicate the general direction of the zoological garden. I believe that I have lost my way.

STANDARD: Could you please tell me how to get to the zoo? I think I'm lost.

INFORMAL: Hey, which way to the zoo? I'm all turned around.

NONSTANDARD: I ain't sure where the zoo is at. I think I'm losted.

Jargon. Jargon is really a type of slang. It's the "inside" language used by people who have the same type of job or share a common interest. Doctors, for example, often speak their own language full of medical jargon that patients can't understand. Every sport has its own jargon, too. For example, the jargon of baseball includes the terms *designated hitter*, *relief pitcher*, *RBI*, *change up*, and *bullpen*. It helps to know something about computers to understand jargon such as *disk drive*, *boot up*, *memory stick*, and *cloud computing*. Astronauts use their own language, too: They use the word *scrub* to mean "cancel a mission," *glitch* is a problem, and a *footprint* is an area where a vehicle can land.

As you can see from these examples, some jargon serves a useful purpose, giving a name to something that didn't have a name before. Jargon also gives people a feeling of togetherness. They can immediately spot someone who shares their interests, because they speak "the same language." The problem comes when jargon-speakers try to communicate with outsiders. Unless they "translate" all the insider terms in their field, those outside the field may have difficulty understanding them. Remember to avoid jargon unless you're talking to someone who shares your interest, or unless you're willing to "translate" the jargon for outsiders.

Euphemisms. In most cases, you should try to avoid using language that might offend your audience. However, some people take this idea much too far. They are so worried about embarrassing or offending other people that they are afraid to use such simple, everyday words as *sweat*, *die*, or *drunk*. Instead they replace these words with euphemisms—pleasant-sounding words for things that people find unpleasant or embarrassing to talk about. They will say *perspiration* rather than *sweat*, for example; *pass away* rather than *die*; and *intoxicated* or *under the influence* rather than *drunk*.

Television commercials are full of euphemisms. You'll seldom hear the words *toilet* or *toilet paper* in a commercial, for example. People in TV commercials worry about cleaning their *bathroom bowls* and buying *bathroom tissue*, instead.

Sometimes advertisers and others use euphemisms to disguise the truth. A *preowned* car sounds more attractive than a *used* or *secondhand* one, for example. People looking for a house quickly learn that anything described as a *handyman's special* is probably a wreck. And when your dentist says you might feel a little *discomfort*, you can usually expect what most of us would refer to as plain old *pain*.

> ಬಿ೧೪
> One day I will find
> the right words,
> and they will
> be simple.
> —Jack Kerouac
> ೮೨ ೧೪

Euphemisms can be used to manipulate public opinion. Naming a new bomb the *Peacemaker*, for example, is a deliberate attempt to persuade people that building more weapons is the way to maintain peace in the world.

Some euphemisms can serve a useful purpose. As you learned in Chapter 5, many words do more than just identify something; they also carry strong connotations. That is, they influence our emotions and encourage us to respond to the thing named in a certain way. Sometimes changing the label we put on people can also change the way we treat them or at least make them feel better about what they do or who they are. If someone would rather be known as a *household worker* than a *maid*, for example, or as a *sanitation worker* rather than a *garbage collector*, that is his or her privilege. And as older people became known as *senior citizens*, they came to be recognized as a group of citizens with special rights and needs.

That old children's rhyme that says "Names can never hurt me" is totally untrue. Words are powerful. They *can* hurt people. The names we give to things and the words we use to talk about issues influence the way we think about them.

Good English Is Concise

Gobbledygook. Most often, a few precise, everyday words can express an idea better than a string of long, important-sounding ones. The use of long, confusing words is known as *gobbledygook*. Like euphemisms, gobbledygook can be used to disguise unpleasant realities. Calling a lie a *strategic misrepresentation*, for example, is an attempt to hide the fact that someone has done something wrong. Many government documents contain examples of this unfortunate tendency. Suppose you read the following sentence, for example:

> A revenue enhancement will be required to implement effective policies to ameliorate the negative impact of atmospheric deposition of anthropogenically-derived acidic substances.

Most people would have no idea what the sentence means. But all it's really saying is:

We'll need to raise taxes to fight acid rain.

People who write advertising copy, which must communicate quickly and effectively, are often given the code word **KISS** to remind them of their goal:

> **K**eep
> **I**t
> **S**imple
> **S**tupid

Of course you shouldn't take the language of commercials as the model for your writing, because advertising is often misleading and manipulative, but the rule about keeping things simple and clear is a good one to remember.

Redundancies. Another way to weed out unnecessary words from your writing is to avoid redundancies—expressions that say the same thing twice. For example, to say that something was *totally destroyed* is redundant, because the word *destroyed* all by itself means totally broken or completely defeated. Other redundant expressions to avoid include:

> important breakthrough (a breakthrough is important by definition)
> refer back (the *re* in *refer* means "back")
> end result
> previous history
> twelve o'clock noon (just *noon* is sufficient)
> combine together
> follow after
> might possibly
> never at any time

Good English Can Be Colorful

Good English shouldn't be dull. Just because you're being correct doesn't mean you have to be boring. If you choose precise nouns and verbs, words that paint vivid pictures (see Chapter 5), then you won't put your audience to sleep.

More About Slang. Is it ever all right to use slang in your writing? Sometimes, especially if you're writing about something current, such as a particular style of music, and you want the subject to come alive. Just be considerate of your audience. If you're writing for someone who doesn't know much about the subject, you'll need to "translate" some terms. And don't overdo it. A little bit of slang can be fun. Too much can wear your reader out or irritate him or her.

Regionalisms. If you have friends or relatives who live in different parts of the United States, or if you've moved around the country yourself, then you know that not all Americans give the same names to certain objects. If you live in the Midwest, for example, you may drink *pop*, but if you live in New York, you drink *soda*, instead. Same thing, different name. These are examples of regionalisms. Regionalisms are fun and interesting. But if you travel or if you write for an audience outside your own area, then it's important to realize your own regionalisms.

NOTE: If you enjoy comparing your own regionalisms to those of people in other parts of the country, you're not alone. Language experts have been studying American regionalisms for years to compile the multivolume and digital *Dictionary of American Regional English* (*DARE*). You may enjoy browsing through it at your local library. You can also find information about *DARE* at http://dare.wisc.edu/, and even enjoy dozens of sample entries.

TRY IT: Identify the word you most often use for the following things. If the regionalism you use for the item is not listed, write it on a separate sheet of paper.

1. a paper container used to carry groceries:
   a. bag
   b. sack
   c. poke

2. what's in the center of a peach:
   a. pit
   b. seed
   c. stone

3. a breakfast treat:
   a. griddlecake
   b. pancake
   c. battercake

4. to deliberately miss school:
   a. play hookey
   b. skip school
   c. blow school

5. a playground ride:
   a. seesaw
   b. teeter-totter
   c. teeterboard

6. your father:
   a. father
   b. dad or daddy
   c. pa or papa or pop

7. a sandwich on a hard roll:
   a. hero
   b. sub
   c. hoagie
   d. grinder
   e. torpedo

8. something on a diagonal from something else:
   a. kitty-corner
   b. catty-corner
   c. cater-corner

9. what you pull on a Thanksgiving turkey:
   a. wishbone

    b. pull bone
    c. lucky bone

10. an object to fry food in:
    a. skillet
    b. frying pan
    c. fry pan
    d. spider

Summary

Remember these rules of good English:

1. *Be clear.* Try to say exactly what you mean by using the most precise words you know.
2. *Be considerate.* If you want to "get through" to an audience, speak their language. Don't use words they won't understand or won't approve of. Follow the rules in situations in which the rules are important.
3. *Be concise.* Say what you need to say in as few words as possible. Don't use strings of long, confusing words to impress people. You'll only confuse your audience and make them frustrated or angry.
4. *Be colorful when appropriate.* Don't be afraid to use lively words and expressions to get your audience's or reader's attention, but don't overdo it or use the words that are inappropriate to the situation.

Chapter 7

The Name's the Same:

A Homonym Glossary

Many people can't take full advantage of the vocabulary they already have, because they don't know how to spell so many of the words they "know." This is especially true when it comes to homonyms, those irritating, everyday words that sound the same, but are spelled differently and have different meanings. Then there are words that sound *almost* alike, which are just as confusing to spell.

If your essays and book reports frequently come back with lots of words marked as misspelled, maybe you should permanently bookmark this chapter and the next for easy reference. That way, you can turn here for help before you hand in your next assignment (or at least after you get the assignment back and it's time to make revisions and corrections).

The rest of this chapter is a glossary of the homonym pairs people often confuse, arranged in alphabetical order. It's better than a dictionary because the two confusing words are listed together, rather than pages apart. In the next chapter, you'll get a list of spelling rules and tips for remembering the spelling of "hard" words.

Homonym Glossary

affect — usually a verb: How will the chances *affect* you?
effect —usually a noun: What *effect* will the changes have
    on you?

ant — the insect
aunt — the relative

ate — past tense of *to eat*
eight — the number

bare — not dressed, without covering
bear — 1) the animal; 2) to endure; 3) to carry

base — 1) what a baseball player runs to; 2) the bottom of
    something
bass — 1) lowest voice in a choir; 2) type of musical
    instrument

be — to exist
bee — the insect

blew — past tense of *to blow*
blue — the color

boarder — tenant
border — boundary
bored — not interested
board — piece of wood

bow — to bend from the waist in respect
bough — part of a tree

brake — what stops the car
break — to smash or to stop working
by — near
buy — opposite of *sell*

choose — to select
chews — bites into pieces

close — opposite of *to open* (Also: opposite of far)
clothes — what you wear

coarse — rough or unrefined
course — 1) route; 2) subject studied in school

complimentary — 1) flattering; 2) free
complementary — describes something that completes,
     enhances, or fits together with something else
     (*complementary* colors, *complementary*
     personalities, *complementary* ideas)

counsel — advice (One who gives advice is a *counselor*)
council — organization

desert (dez′ ərt) — a dry place
desert (də zurt′) — to abandon
dessert (də zurt′) — what you have at the end of a meal

die — to stop living
dye — something used to transfer color

fair — 1) just; 2) festival or carnival; 3) clear and sunny;
     4) light-colored
fare — cost of public transportation

A Homonym Glossary

flour — what bread is made of
flower — rose, daisy, etc.

forth — forward
fourth — comes after third

great — large or wonderful
grate — to shred into small pieces

hear — what you do with your ear
here — at this place

hoarse — losing one's voice
horse — the animal

hole — hollowed out place or opening
whole — entire, all of something

its — belonging to it
it's — contraction for *it is*

led — past tense of *to lead*
lead — a heavy metal

loose (loōs) — opposite of *tight*
lose (loōz) — 1) opposite of *to win*; 2) opposite of *to find*

mail — letters, packages, etc.
male — opposite of *female*

new — opposite of *old*
knew — past tense of *to know*

night — opposite of *day*
knight — warrior of the Middle Ages

no — opposite of *yes*
know — to understand, realize

our — belonging to us
hour — 60 minutes

pail — container, another word for *bucket*
pale — light in color

pain — discomfort
pane — sheet of glass

passed — past tense of *to pass* (I *passed* the test. We
        passed the car.)
past — 1) not in the present; 2) beyond (Go *past* the bank
        and turn left.)

peace — opposite of war
piece — part of the whole, a single thing

plain — 1) not fancy; 2) level country; 3) clear, obvious
plane — 1) short form of *airplane*; 2) dimension, flat
        surface; 3) two-dimensional; 4) to make smooth or
        level

pray — to say a prayer
prey — 1) to hunt down or take advantage of; 2) an animal
        that is hunted by another

principal — 1) head of a school; 2) first in importance
principle — basic idea, belief, or law

A Homonym Glossary

rain — water that falls from the sky
rein — part of the equipment used to ride horses
reign — the time that a king or queen rules

real — actual
reel — 1) spool of film; 2) a dance; 3) to stagger

red — the color
read — past tense of *to read*

right — 1) opposite of *left*; 2) opposite of *wrong*
write — to put words on paper

roll — 1) kind of bread or pastry; 2) to turn over and over;
     3) list of names for taking attendance
role — part played by an actor

sea — body of water
see — what you do with your eyes

seam — where two pieces of fabric are sewn together
seem — to appear

seen — past tense of *to see*
scene — part of a play

sell — opposite of *to buy*
cell — 1) smallest unit of all living things; 2) battery; 3) a
     type of telephone

seller — one who sells
cellar — basement

A Homonym Glossary

sent — past tense of *to send*
cent — penny, 1/100 of a dollar
scent — smell

sense — logic
cents — more than one cent

sight — vision, what is seen
site — location
cite — to mention or refer to

shone — past tense of *to shine*
shown — past participle of *to show*

so — common word with various meanings, including
　　　therefore (I was tired *so* I went to bed.), *to a great
　　　degree* (I was *so* tired.), etc.
sew — to use a needle and thread
sow — to plant seeds

soar — to fly
sore — painful, especially from overuse

stake — 1) pointed object used to secure a tent; 2) an item
　　　or amount of money wagered; 3) a person's share of
　　　interest in something
steak — type of meat

stair — step, part of a staircase
stare — to look at something steadily, with great
　　　concentration

stationary — unmoving
stationery — writing paper

steal — to rob
steel — hard metal made from iron

sum — total
some — not all

sun — Earth's source of light and heat
son — a parent's male child

tail — what a dog wags
tale — story
taut — tight
taught — past tense of *to teach*

tax — money paid by citizens to their government
tacks — small pointed objects used to attach paper to a
      bulletin board, etc.

tea — liquid served hot or iced
tee — tiny platform on which a golf ball is placed

their — belonging to them
they're — contraction for *they are*
there — opposite of *here*

then — at that time, used to tell when something hap-
      pened
than — used to make comparisons (better *than* the rest)

threw — past tense of *to throw*
through — 1) finished; 2) in one side and out the other

throne — where a king or queen sits
thrown — past participle of *to throw*

A Homonym Glossary

to — the preposition: I went *to* the store. Give it *to* me.

two — the number

too — 1) also (I want to go, *too*.); 2) overly (That music is
   too slow.)

toe — what you have five of on each foot

tow — to pull

vain — conceited

vein — what your blood flows through

vane — something that shows which way the wind is blow-
   ing

waist — the part of your body you put a belt around

waste — to use up something unwisely, to not take full
   advantage of something (Also, garbage, refuse)

wait — what impatient people find hard to do

weight — what you step on a scale to find out

way — path or method

weigh — to put on a scale

weak — opposite of strong

week — seven days

wear — 1) to have something on the body; 2) to be slowly
   used up or diminished over time

where — at what place?

weather — atmospheric conditions

whether — if

wood — material that comes from a tree
would — used to express a condition (I *would* help him if I
      could.)

your — belonging to you
you're— *you are*

whose — belonging to whom? (*Whose* jacket is this?)
who's — contraction of *who is* (*Who's* coming with me?)

Try It: Which Witch Is Which?
You could use the homonyms in the title above to ask a
question if you were confused at a Halloween party. Each
of the following questions can be answered by a pair of
homonyms. How many can you spell correctly? The first
one has been done for you.

1. What two homonyms are another way of saying a light-
   colored bucket? A _pale_ _pail_

2. What two homonyms mean to abandon the sweets that
   are served at the end of a meal? To _____
   _____

3. Jim said, "I'm changing my seat and moving up to the
   front because I can't _____ what people are
   saying from way back _____."

4. To send a boy in an envelope would be to _____
   a _____.

5. To note down something correctly would be to
   _____ it _____.

6. To look intently at a step is to _____ at a
   _____.

7. How much _____ _____ a woodchuck
   chuck if a woodchuck could chuck _____?

Chapter 8

Write it Right:

Improving Your Spelling

Why a chapter on spelling in a vocabulary book? Well, say you put a lot of effort into an essay for English class. You come up with a brilliant idea, you organize your thoughts carefully, and you spend a lot of time selecting just the right words—the ones that say precisely what you mean. You're convinced that this time you've come up with a winning combination and written something you can be proud of—but the essay comes back with red marks all over it and comments from the teacher about your carelessness.

After all your hard work, you've failed to communicate, and your teacher has gotten the wrong impression of your attitude toward your work. Unfair? It may seem that way, but put yourself in your teacher's shoes (for just a second!). It's hard to appreciate someone's ideas when you have to struggle to make out misspelled words in every sentence. And it's difficult to give someone credit for care and precision when the first thing you notice is the person's carelessness and lack of precision about spelling.

That doesn't mean that people who spell well and easily are necessarily smarter than people who don't. There have been famous writers who were poor spellers. But, unfortunately, most of us aren't famous geniuses. We don't have editors and secretaries to correct all our embarrassing mistakes. And we can't expect our teachers, friends, or bosses to think it's a pleasure to spend hours deciphering what we *meant* to say. So it's a smart idea to try to improve our spelling.

Good Spellers are More Confident about Words

Improving your spelling can also give you more confidence about using words. Once you have a picture of a word in your mind, you're more likely to use it. Poor spellers sometimes think of great words to use, but they get so frustrated trying to spell them that they settle for words that are not quite as good but easier to spell, instead. Don't let poor spelling keep you from doing your best.

How to Improve Your Spelling

Learn the rules. Everyone knows that English is a difficult language to spell, but there are some rules that can help (honest!). They won't help you with every word, but they will enable you to avoid some common spelling pitfalls. You'll find the most important spelling rules you need to remember in the Spelling Rules section of this book. Mark this section of the book and refer to it when you need help.

Take pictures of words as you read. Careful readers are often good spellers. They can close their eyes and "see" words in their mind because they've "taken pictures" of them as they read. Some people are better at this skill than others, but you can improve your ability by practicing. Try it. If you look at a word and see it in your mind often enough, it may start to look "funny" when you spell it wrong.

Notice spelling "hot spots." Some words have built-in trouble spots that are like traps set for careless spellers. Double letters and silent letters are two examples. Look out for these traps. When you notice one, take a picture of the word and then *tell* yourself about the problem—actually *say* to yourself, for example, "Don't forget the double *l's* in *parallel*" or, "Don't forget the *secret* in *secretary*."

You'll find lots of practice with spelling "hot spots" in the Spelling Demons section of this chapter.

Use your dictionary or ask a good speller for help. It's true that it's not always easy to look up the spelling of a word you don't know how to spell! But it can be done. You just have to try different variations on how you think the word *might* be spelled, and hope one of your ideas is right. When all else fails, *ask someone for help*, preferably a good speller. Then confirm what the person tells you by looking up the word in the dictionary. (Even good spellers occasionally make mistakes.) Proofread all your written work before you hand it in, and look up the spelling of any word you're not sure of.

Start your own spelling glossary. Most of us misspell the same words over and over again. There are certain words we just draw a blank on, no matter how many times we try to picture them in our minds or tell ourselves the trouble spots to look out for. Keep a list of your own personal spelling demons in a special notebook or file on your computer. When you misspell a word or have to look it up, enter the correct spelling in your spelling glossary. Then you can refer to the glossary first when you proofread your work. Assuming there will be fewer words listed there than in the dictionary, it will be easier to look up the words you frequently misspell.

Use spell-check carefully. Spell-checking functions built into word processing programs, whether for use on computers, smart phones, or other electronic devices, can be a big help, but they can also hinder writers and cause them to make mistakes. This is especially true in the case of homonyms, which you learned about in Chapter 7. For example, spell-check did not detect the mistakes in either of the following sentences:

> When it began to rein, we decided to stay home and watch a movie.
> She paid me a very nice complement about my dress.

On the other hand, spell-check successfully detected the mistakes in these sentences:

> I had to weight a long time for the train because it was late.
> There were fore or five other passengers waiting.

These examples demonstrate that spell-check is not necessarily a writer's dream when it comes to spelling. It is inconsistent and unpredictable, so careful proofreading is still a key requirement for putting your best foot forward as a writer.

Spelling Rules
USING IE AND EI
If the sound is long *e*, put *i* before *e*—except after *c*.

I before E

piece	chief
niece	brief
field	thief
yield	grief
shield	relief
fierce	relieve

pierce	achieve
siege	believe

Except after C

receive	deceive
receipt	deceit
perceive	conceited
ceiling	

Exceptions: either, neither, weird, seize, leisure
If the sound is not long *e*, put *e* before *i*.

E before I

sleigh	vein
neigh	veil
neighbor	their
weigh	height
weight	Fahrenheit
freight	forfeit
rein	counterfeit
reign	foreign
reindeer	

Exceptions: friend, mischief, mischievous, sieve

ADDING A PREFIX
When adding a prefix to a word, don't add or drop any letters. Just combine the prefix and the word. If the last letter of the prefix and the first letter of the original word are the same, the combined word will have a double letter.

dis + appear = *dis*appear
dis + appoint = *dis*appoint
dis + approve = *dis*approve
dis + agree = *dis*agree
dis + satisfied = *dis*satisfied

dis + service = *dis*service
dis + similar = *dis*similar
mis + apply = *mis*apply
mis + adventure = *mis*adventure
mis + step = *mis*step
mis + spell = *mis*spell
im + practical = *im*practical
im + mature = *im*mature
il + legal = *il*legal
un + inhabited = *un*inhabited
un + necessary = *un*necessary

ADDING THE SUFFIXES -NESS AND -LY

When adding the suffixes *-ness* and *-ly*, don't drop or change any letters in the original word, unless the word ends in y (see CHANGING Y TO I). If the first letter of the suffix and the last letter of the original word are the same, the new word will have a double letter.

sad + ness = sad*ness*
stubborn + ness = stubborn*ness*
mean + ness = mean*ness*
sudden + ness = sudden*ness*
final + ly = final*ly*
usual + ly = usual*ly*
real + ly = real*ly*
incidental + ly = incidental*ly*
occasional + ly = occasional*ly*
natural + ly = natural*ly*
general + ly = general*ly*
beautiful + ly = beautiful*ly*

Exception: For words ending in *ic*, add *-ally* instead of just *-ly*.

    realistic + ally = realistic*ally*
    pathetic + ally = pathetic*ally*
    democratic + ally = democratic*ally*
    enthusiastic + ally = enthusiastic*ally*
    energetic + ally = energetic*ally*

DROPPING SILENT E

For words ending in silent *e*, drop the *e* before adding a suffix that begins with a vowel, but keep the *e* when adding a suffix that begins with a consonant.

    retire + ment = retire*ment*
    retire + ing = retir*ing*
    retrieve + able = retriev*able*
    care + ful = care*ful*
    care + ing = car*ing*
    value + able = valu*able*
    insure + ance = insur*ance*

Exceptions: argument, truly, judgment
Other Exceptions: When the word ends in *ce* or *ge*, KEEP the silent *e* before suffixes beginning with *a* or *o*.

    courage + ous = courage*ous*
    replace + able = replace*able*

CHANGING Y TO I

For words ending in *y* preceded by a consonant, change the *y* to *i* before adding any suffix except *-ing*. Keep the y when adding *-ing*.

    rely + able = rel*iable*
    rely + ing = rel*ying*

happy + ly = happ*ily*
happy + er = happ*ier*
happy + ness = happ*iness*
hurry + ed = hurr*ied*
hurry + ing = hurr*ying*
study + ed = stud*ied*
study + ing = stud*ying*

For words ending in *y* preceded by a vowel, do NOT change *y* to *i* before a suffix.

destroy + er = destro*yer*
convey + ed = conve*yed*

DOUBLING CONSONANTS
For one-syllable words ending in a single consonant preceded by a single vowel, double the final consonant before adding a suffix that begins with a vowel.

shop + ing = sho*pping*
trap + ed = tra*pped*
swim + er = swi*mmer*

For words of more than one syllable, double the final consonant ONLY if the words meets ALL of the following requirements:

1. The original word ends with a single consonant preceded by a single vowel.
2. The original word is accented on the last syllable. (Accented syllables are indicated by **bold** type below.)
3. You are adding a suffix that begins with a vowel.
4. After you add the suffix, the word is still accented on the same syllable.

begin + ing = beginning
admit + ed = admitted
occur + ence = occurrence
forget + able = forgettable
refer + al = referral
profit + ed = **prof**ited (Accent is on first syllable. Do NOT double consonant.)
benefit + ing = **ben**efiting (Accent is on first syllable. Do NOT double consonant.)
prefer + ed = preferred (double consonant)
prefer + ence = preference (Accent changes in new word. Do NOT double consonant.)
equip + ed = **equipped** (double consonant)
equip + ment = **equip**ment (Suffix does not begin with a vowel, so do NOT double consonant.)

ADDING K AFTER IC
For words ending in *ic*, add a *k* before adding the suffixes
-er, *-ed*, *-ing*, or *-y*.

panic + ed = panicked
panic + y = panicky
picnic + ing = picnicking

PLURALS
To form the plural of most nouns, add *s*.

desk—desks
ghost—ghosts
bike—bikes

For a word ending in *s*, *ch*, *sh*, *x*, or *z*, ad *es*.

glass—glass*es*
match—match*es*
crash—crash*es*
ax—ax*es*
waltz—waltz*es*

For nouns ending in *y* preceded by a consonant, change *y* to *i* and add *es*. If *y* is preceded by a vowel, just add *s*.

sky—sk*ies*
comedy—comed*ies*
baby—bab*ies*
duty—du*ties*
tray—tray*s*
boy—boy*s*

For some words ending in *o* preceded by a consonant, add *es* to form the plural. For others, just add *s*. For nouns ending in *o* preceded by a vowel, always just add *s*. Memorize this list.

hero—hero*es*
echo—echo*es*
tomato—tomato*es*
potato—potato*es*
tornado—tornado*es*
banjo—banjo*s*
piano—piano*s*
soprano—soprano*s*
video—video*s*
radio—radio*s*

For some words ending in *f* or *fe*, just add s to form the plural. For others, change the *f* or *fe* to *v* and add *es*. Memorize these lists.

chief–chiefs	knife–kni*ves*	half–hal*ves*
belief–beliefs	life–li*ves*	self–sel*ves*
safe–safes	loaf–loa*ves*	leaf–lea*ves*
roof–roofs	wife–wi*ves*	wolf–wol*ves*
	calf–cal*ves*	thief–thie*ves*

Some plurals are spelled in special ways. Memorize them.

woman—women
man—men
child—children
mouse—mice
foot—feet
tooth—teeth
goose—geese

Finally, some plurals are spelled exactly the same as the singular.

deer—deer
moose—moose
fish—fish (fishes is also correct)
aircraft—aircraft
you—you
pants—pants
shorts—shorts
eyeglasses—eyeglasses
scissors—scissors
species—species
offspring—offspring

Spelling Demons

As you've probably noticed, many English words are not spelled the way they are pronounced. That's why you need more than rules to help you become a good speller. The truth is that to spell words correctly, you need to pay close

> If you can spell "Nietzsche" without Google, you deserve a cookie.
> –Lauren Leto

attention to them as you read, memorize the way they look, and practice spelling them until the correct spellings seem natural. It's not easy, but there's a way to make it a little easier. There are certain words that many people misspell over and over again—and for very good reasons! In this section, these spelling "demons" are grouped according to the reasons that people usually misspell them. The "danger area" of each word is underlined. By studying words with similar "problems" together, as a group, you may be able to remember them better. It's worth a try, right?

See how many of these words you can spell correctly after looking them over briefly. Cover one word at a time with a piece of paper, and try writing it out in a notebook or on your keyboard. Keep track of the ones you get right.

Once you've tried all the spelling demons, go back and see which words you missed. If you want, copy the words correctly into your own "Personal Spelling Glossary" in a special notebook or electronic file. Set it up so that it is in alphabetical order for easy reference. That way, you'll have your own personal spelling dictionary when you're finished. You can use your personal dictionary to check for spelling errors before handing in class assignments. And you can add more words to the dictionary as you get back your graded papers. Good luck!

DON'T ADD UNNECESSARY LETTERS TO THESE WORDS:

athletic (*not* atheletic)
disastrous (*not* disasterous)
drowned (*not* drownded)
entrance (*not* enterance)
height (*not* heighth)
hindrance (*not* hinderance)
lightning (*not* lightening)
mischievous (*not* mischievious)
wintry (*not* wintery)

DON'T LEAVE OUT IMPORTANT LETTERS IN THESE WORDS:

arctic	liberal
boundary	literature
candidate	memory
desperate	miniature
different	ordinary
environment	probably
favorably	privilege
favorite	quantity
identify	recognize
interest	representative
interference	several
library	surprise

NOTICE THE SILENT LETTERS IN THESE WORDS:

business	listen
chocolate	parliament
condemn	psychology
excellent	prisoner

elementary
exhausted
exhilarated
fasten
fiery
laboratory

resign
sophomore
strength
temperature
temperament
Wednesday

NOTICE THE DOUBLE LETTERS IN THESE WORDS:

bookkeeper
accommodate
address
aggressive
assassin
balloon
accelerate
accomplish
accumulate
assistant
broccoli
cinnamon
collaborate
colossal
dilemma
disappoint
exaggerate
excellent
fulfill

committee
commission
embarrass
occurrence
possession
raccoon
interrupt
mayonnaise
moccasin
miscellaneous
necessary
occasional
parallel
professor
questionnaire
recommend
satellite
spaghetti
tyranny

NOTICE WHAT LETTER MAKES THE "UH" SOUND IN EACH WORD:

comparative
separate
vanilla
academy
benefit

illustrate
design
device
mathematics
phenomenon

category
celebrate
competition
delegate
despair
describe
authority
comparison
classify
confidential
criticize
definite
discussion
divide
dividend
eligible
eliminate
estimate
imaginary
imitate
legitimate
magnify
alcohol
monotonous

relevant
repetition
vinegar
medicine
modify
optimism
preliminary
primitive
priority
prominent
quality
responsibility
sensible
sensibility
sensitive
significant
simplify
specimen
spiritual
unanimous
philosophy
proposition
illustrate
design

NOTICE WORDS ENDING IN *-ANT* (OR *-ANCE*) AND *-ENT* (OR *-ENCE*)

ant or ance:

abundance
appearance
attendance
attendant
descendant

instance
irrelevant
relevance
resistance

ent or ence:

confid*ent*	independ*ent*
confid*ence*	independ*ence*
correspond*ence*	insist*ent*
depend*ent*	persist*ence*
depend*ence*	sent*ence*
exist*ence*	superintend*ent*

-ISE and *-IZE*

Most words with the īz sound end in *-ize*. Memorize these exceptions that end in *-ise*. Notice that many of them end in *-vise*.

advert*ise*	exerc*ise*
comprom*ise*	improv*ise*
disgu*ise*	rev*ise*
dev*ise*	superv*ise*
enterpr*ise*	surpr*ise*

Note: Two common words end in *-yze* and have related forms that end in *-ysis*.

analy*ze* – analy*sis*
paraly*ze* – paraly*sis*

-ABLE and *-IBLE*

Memorize the ends of the following words. (Note: There are really more words that end in *-able*, but the *-ible* ones are more often misspelled.)

accept*able*	collaps*ible*	horr*ible*
depend*able*	combust*ible*	incred*ible*
indispens*able*	compat*ible*	irresist*ible*

inevit<u>able</u>	convert<u>ible</u>	leg<u>ible</u>
insepar<u>able</u>	corrupt<u>ible</u>	plaus<u>ible</u>
irrit<u>able</u>	elig<u>ible</u>	poss<u>ible</u>
predict<u>able</u>	ed<u>ible</u>	revers<u>ible</u>
	flex<u>ible</u>	suscept<u>ible</u>
	gull<u>ible</u>	terr<u>ible</u>
		vis<u>ible</u>

-ER or *-OR*

Memorize these words that end in *-or* rather than in *-er*:

accelerat<u>or</u>	impost<u>or</u>
ancest<u>or</u>	indicat<u>or</u>
commentat<u>or</u>	invest<u>or</u>
contribut<u>or</u>	investigat<u>or</u>
distribut<u>or</u>	supervis<u>or</u>
edit<u>or</u>	surviv<u>or</u>
elevat<u>or</u>	spectat<u>or</u>
escalat<u>or</u>	visit<u>or</u>

CEED, SEDE, and SEDE

Only one word ends in <u>sede</u>: super<u>sede</u>.
Only three words end in <u>ceed</u>: suc<u>ceed</u>, ex<u>ceed</u>, pro<u>ceed</u>.
Most words with this ending sound end in <u>cede</u>:

con<u>cede</u>	pre<u>cede</u>	se<u>cede</u>
inter<u>cede</u>	re<u>cede</u>	

Parting Words

Words are Alive

If you've ever told a joke, you know that words can be fun. If you've ever had an argument with a friend or relative, you that words can hurt. Words can connect us to other people—or drive people apart. Words can make people understand—or confuse them. The words that we have stored in our brains determine *what* we can think about—and *how* we can think about things. Words are alive. They can reflect our deepest thoughts and feelings, our most secret hopes and fears.

So often in school we forget how close we really are to words. They suddenly seem unnatural, unnecessary, unconnected to what we really think and feel, to what really matters to us. That's a shame.

> I still believe in the power of the word, that words inspire.
> — Joni Mitchell

Do It for Yourself

Don't learn about words to please your parents or your teachers. Do it for yourself. Knowing about words means being able to think more clearly, to understand what you are feeling, and to make connections with other people.

To get good grades, of course, you have to think about pleasing your teachers. But try to imagine what *you* can get out of each assignment. When you write an essay, choose a topic that interests you and imagine you're writing to someone who really matters to you, and who really cares about what you have to say. Try to find *something* that you can get out of each assignment, even if it's the small satisfaction of having finished something you no longer have to worry about.

> ഇരു
>
> All of my life I've looked at words as though I were seeing them for the first time.
> —Ernest Hemingway
>
> ഇരു

Pay Attention

Whenever you read or listen, pay attention to the words people use. How are words used to paint a picture, to make people laugh, or to stir deep emotions? Is the language clear, considerate, concise, and colorful? Or is it confusing, offensive, boring, or manipulative? How do the ways that other people use language relate to things that *you'd* like to say, and ways *you'd* like to say them?

Think of English as something that belongs to you, something that gives you power and enjoyment. Take charge of your words and make them accomplish things for you in your world.

INDEX